"Technology is almost omnipresent whether we like it or not. So what do we do with this thing that is impacting people everywhere? Very few Christians think a lot about this, but John Dyer has. In a balanced journey through the digital world, he shows us what to like and be aware of about our technological world. *From the Garden to the City* is more than a trip through the digital world; it is a tour of discovery about a growing part of our lives. Read and discover what technology is and can be."

—**Darrell Bock**, author of *Jesus According to Scripture*

"We all have a great deal of experience with technology, but few of us have sought to think about technology in a distinctly Christian way. This is one reason I commend John Dyer's *From the Garden to the City*. As comfortable with theology as he is with technology, Dyer is a steady guide to the digital world we find ourselves in."

—**Tim Challies**, author of *The Next Story: Life and Faith After the Digital Explosion*

"Slow down for a minute; be still and ponder what John Dyer is addressing in this helpful book. Technology is undeniably reshaping how we communicate with, relate to, and ultimately love one another. If you've ever texted, tweeted, or sent an email to someone who was sitting right next to you at the time, you're affected. It's time for you to read *From the Garden to the City*."

—**Bob Lepine**, cohost of *FamilyLife Today*

"It's odd that most of us spend our days immersed in and preoccupied with technology, yet also take its most important features entirely for granted. This book is full of jewels of observation that will help you see technology, the Bible, and your own life afresh. It's frequently funny, surprisingly moving, and consistently smart—a great guide for those who want to begin thinking about how technology shapes us and how we can live faithfully with it."

—**Andy Crouch**, author of *Culture Making: Recovering Our Creative Calling*

"John is the unusual person who is as expert in information technology as he is familiar with the Bible, and he is even more unusual in being able to move to and fro with ease and come up with striking and helpful insights. His voice, though gentle, speaks with authority."

—**Albert Borgmann**, author of *Real American Ethics*

"John Dyer has essentially written the book I've always wanted to write except he's executed it with far more excellence and comprehension than I am capable of! John has created a superbly crafted theological framework for both the layperson and technology enthusiast, so they both can engage wisely, rejoicing in technology's redeeming properties while being cautious with the corruptive. John balances the contemporary challenges that newer devices create with timeless historical models from the Scriptures that give answers that more than satisfy. Thanks, John, for giving this fast-paced generation something worthy enough to cause us to pause, realign, and reprogram our thinking for not only ourselves but all those that we impact in our relationships, businesses, and ministries. I will never look at my iPhone the same way again, and I'm a better person for it—and you will be too."

—**John Saddington**, Professional Blogger, TentBlogger.com

"John Dyer does a magnificent job—the best that I have seen—of explaining to the Christian community how and why technology *cannot* be morally neutral. He crafts his arguments carefully, using examples from his field of information and computer technology (insiders use the term *computer-mediated communications*). But the principles he extracts are quite general and include fresh insights into the role of technology in culture and matters of the spirit. Perhaps his greatest contribution is that he shows contemporary Western culture to be determined by technology as much or more than by any other force. That insight may come as something of a shock to the musicians, poets, philosophers, and media producers to whom the Church has attributed the role of culture-formers. Especially, however, it creates a new challenge for pastors and church leaders who now must add discernment of technology to their teaching about popular culture. . . .

From the Garden to the City contains several fresh and fascinating new insights."

—**Jack Clayton Swearengen,** Emeritus Professor of Engineering at Washington State University, nuclear weapon scientist, and author of *Beyond Paradise: Technology and the Kingdom of God*

"It's a unique perspective that combines the heart of a theologian with the brain of a high-tech expert, but that's what you get with John Dyer. And speaking as a pastor, I believe that's what *you* need as well if you share in any sort of spiritual leadership. Our cause is to live and communicate the good news as deeply and as broadly as we can, using all the tools at our disposal, especially and including high-tech tools. But as John shows, we must be wise in the use of technology lest we and our cause change to serve it and not the other way around. *From the Garden to the City* offers biblical, profound, and practical insights as to how we can do just that."

—**Dr. Andy McQuitty**, pastor of Irving Bible Church, Irving, Texas

"There are few guides through the sometimes uneasy relationship between technology and Christianity that I would more highly commend than John Dyer. In this book, he walks us through difficult concepts in ways that are eminently accessible. Never hysterical but appropriately critical, *From the Garden to the City* provides an important and timely framework for churches and leaders to think through how they can use technology without technology using them."

—**Matthew Lee Anderson**, author of *Earthen Vessels*

FROM THE
GARDEN
TO THE CITY

THE REDEEMING AND CORRUPTING
POWER OF TECHNOLOGY

JOHN DYER
Foreword by Dr. T. David Gordon

Kregel
Publications

Published by Kregel Publications, a division of Kregel, Inc., P.O. Box 2607, Grand Rapids, MI 49501.

Library of Congress Cataloging-in-Publication Data
Dyer, John.
    From the garden to the city : the redeeming and corrupting power of technology / John Dyer.
       p. cm.
    Includes bibliographical references and index.
    1. Technology—Religious aspects—Christianity. I. Title.
BR115.T42D94   2011   261.5'6—dc22   2011013589

ISBN 978-0-8254-2668-1

Printed in the United States of America

11 12 13 14 15 / 5 4 3 2 1

To Amber,
who taught me
Heidegger, laughter, and
unmediated love

CONTENTS

FOREWORD

John Dyer has written a book that few could write. Trained both in information technology and in theology, and well-versed in media ecology, he is unusually qualified to raise questions about how we make tools and how tools make us, focusing especially on the more recent developments in electronic and image-based technologies. With his distinctive background, Dyer is able to ask and answer two questions of our tools and technologies: What do they do *for* us? And, What do they do *to* us?

Dyer's viewpoint is self-consciously Christian without being reactionary, tech-savvy without being naive, and well-considered without being pedantic. At a moment in history when our tools are being developed at a rate faster than our capacity to evaluate their impact, we need reliable guides to help us to understand them well, so that we can use them thoughtfully and intentionally. John Dyer is such a guide; and this insightful volume dodges none of the difficult questions, while retaining a balanced and judicious consideration of those areas that do not yet enjoy universal consensus.

From the Garden to the City traces the history of technology and tool-making from a distinctively Christian point of view; and candidly acknowledges that both human wisdom and folly, both piety and impiety, both humility and pride, have contributed chapters to this complicated history. Neither technophobes nor technophiles will be entirely satisfied with either Dyer's judicious reasoning or his cautionary encouragements. Each will prefer total, apocalyptic warfare, and each will be uncomfortable with his sniperlike precision.

I have looked for a volume like this since I began teaching an introduction to media ecology class almost a decade ago; and I commend it to all who are interested in electronic and image-based technologies, and to all whose thinking (like mine) has been influenced by people such as Walter Lippmann, Jacques Ellul, Marshall McLuhan, Daniel Boorstin, Walter Ong, Neil Postman, Winifred Gallagher, Maggie Jackson, Maryanne Wolf, Mark Bauerlein, William Powers, and Nicholas Carr.

For all those who desire to be wise and faithful followers of Christ without returning to his moment in technological history, this will prove to be a valuable, if not cherished, guide.

Dr. T. David Gordon
Professor of Religion and Greek
Grove City College
Grove City, PA

ACKNOWLEDGMENTS

For getting this book off the ground, I'd like to thank Frank Barnett, who encouraged me to start a blog after I emailed a few rants about technology several years ago. I'd also like to thank the BibleTech Conference that let me do a talk in 2009, Justin Taylor who posted that talk on his blog, and Ed Komoszewski from Kregel, who saw the talk and then badgered me into submitting a proposal for this book.

While writing, numerous friends offered their encouragement, including my longtime friend Dave Furman, who somehow manages to be rather immediate even half a world away. Thanks also to the men in my small group, each of whom contributed something to this work: Barry Jones (culture), Jeff Taylor (music), Trey Hill (images), Josh Weise (typography), Brady Black (faith), Christian Hemberger (presence), and Dale Dunns (advocacy). Also, thanks to my writing and blogging friends both near and far, Matthew Lee Anderson, Rhett Smith, Scott McClellan, John Saddington, Tim Challies, and the rest. Thanks also to Dallas Theological Seminary, which gave me a wonderful biblical education, and to my boss, Mark Yarbrough, who gave me time to write this book.

A special word of thanks is also due to Dr. Albert Borgmann and Dr. T. David Gordon, both of whom allowed me to ask them questions as I wrote and whose work has been enormously helpful to me and others.

I am indebted to those who took the time to read early versions of this book and offered helpful feedback, especially Adam Keiper of the *New Atlantis*.

I am also grateful for a wonderful family, including my mother, who raised me to be a person hopefully capable of writing a book someone (other than her) would read, and my father, who bought that first Apple IIe. To my dear sister, Ruthie, and my trusted brothers, David and Stephen, I hope our children are blessed with siblings as wonderful as you.

And to my lovely, brilliant wife, Amber, thank you for waiting. Are you free Friday night?

INTRODUCTION

One day, a guest speaker brought an interesting contraption to our church. As our pastor introduced him, he pulled an old reel-to-reel movie projector out of its case and began to set it up. Some of the audience seemed to wonder why he'd bring something so technologically backward, but I was mesmerized as he attached the reels and weaved the celluloid film through a half dozen channels and pulleys. After working with it for some time, he finally connected the film to the second reel, plugged it in, and flipped the switch, but then . . . click, click, click, click . . .

Nothing happened. Something was obviously wrong.

As the clicking sound continued, the room started to grow a little tense. People shifted awkwardly in their seats, letting our guest know he was wasting their time.

But not me. I wasn't bored at all, because I could see exactly what had gone wrong.

So I got up from my chair and marched straight down the aisle of the church, past the guest speaker, and up to the ancient, malfunctioning device. Without saying a word, I began to dismantle what he had done and started to carefully rethread the film back through the correct channels.

The audience watched with some surprise, apparently aware that I had never used this device before. Some shook their heads in disbelief, while others shot knowing grins at each other. I continued to work, slowly threading the film, then reattaching it to the second reel. I checked the plug, flipped a few switches, and then pressed the power button . . . whiiiirrrr . . . it worked!

Now, this story probably seems fairly ordinary. Tech people like me are always fixing things in churches. However, you might be interested to know that I have absolutely no memory of the events I've just described. The only reason I know it happened is that while I was growing up, whenever my mom met someone new, she liked to tell the story of how her three-year-old son had fixed a film projector he had never seen before.

And so began my love and fascination with all things technological, from mechanical projectors to radio control cars and planes to computers and mobile devices. I was the kind of kid who asked for a chemistry set for Christmas so I could do experiments in the garage, and who saved up money for an electronics kit from Radio Shack so I could wire up an alarm for my bedroom. Of course, like most children of the '80s, I played countless hours of video games, but when I finally bought an Xbox, it was not so much because I wanted to play Xbox games but because I wanted to solder in a modchip and play around with home-brew software.

Fast-forward a few decades. As a young adult, I found that I loved doing two things. The first was teaching the Bible, which led me to attend seminary. The second was computer programming, which led me to work in the web development world. God graciously provided me a web design job at the seminary I was attending, allowing me to combine my love for God and his church with my love for technology.

As exciting as it was to do technology work for a ministry, I soon found that working for a ministry does not always pay all the bills. So I took on a few side projects that allowed me to build tools for companies like Apple, Microsoft, Harley Davidson, Anheuser-Busch, the Department of Defense, and Dallas's NPR affiliate.

Throughout my years in seminary, I continued to study and work hard in both theological studies and programming. I spent as much time learning Greek and Hebrew as I did learning languages like PHP, C#, Python, HTML, and JavaScript.

But in my final semester of seminary, a professor, who was known both for his brilliance and shocking, out-of-nowhere statements, said something that changed everything for me. In the middle of addressing a variety of current issues in society and culture, he looked straight at all of us and said, "One of the most dangerous things you can believe in this world is that technology is neutral."

Wait, what? I thought. Surely, he must have misspoken.

After all, nothing could be more obvious than the fact that technology is neutral. What matters is that we *use* technology for good, right?

As he kept talking, I started arguing with the professor in my head. I could not think of a single tool, device, or technology that was morally good or evil in and of itself. Yes, a tool like the nuclear bomb has been used to kill hundreds of thousands of people; but it is based on technology that can also be used to generate inexpensive electricity for millions of people.

Sure, people can choose to abuse computers and the Internet, using them for all kinds of illicit purposes, from identity theft to the distribution of pornography. But the reason I chose web development for an occupation was that I also know the Internet can be used for incredible good. Outside work hours, I built websites to help church leaders find good biblical resources. My entire goal was to use the latest and greatest technology for the good of Christ and his Church.

What could be so dangerous about that?

I returned to class the next day prepared to ask the professor about his statement, armed with the best arguments I could muster about why technology is, in fact, neutral. However, when I arrived that day, the professor was not there. He had fallen ill and would not be able to return to class that semester.

What was I to do? How could I be sure if I was right? And what if the professor was right after all? What if there was some problem with technology that I had never considered? Does the Bible actually say anything about technology? Can we say anything more profound or helpful about our technological world than simply, "Don't be evil" (Google's informal corporate motto)?

So I headed straight for my computer and started scouring the Internet for resources. Strangely though, when I attempted to find specifically Christian reflection on technology, I found very little. A quick search on the Internet for "theology and technology" turned up dozens of results on how to *use* technology. But beyond calls to "redeem technology," I found very little on a biblical position for technology or anything about how technology fits into the redemptive story told in the Scriptures.

Just as I was about to give up in frustration, a dear friend who works two floors up from my office gave me a book on Marshall McLuhan's thought, and another friend who lives halfway around the world gave me a book by Neil Postman, a student of McLuhan. I later found out that McLuhan and Postman founded an academic discipline called media ecology, which studies how technology operates within cultures and how it changes them over time. Media ecologists look at what happens when a technology enters a culture the same way that a biologist examines what happens when a new animal species enters an ecological environment.

Digging a bit more, I found a subdiscipline of philosophy called—obviously enough—"philosophy of technology," which asks questions about how technology relates to what it means to be human. These questions include "Does technology have an independent nature?" and "Should humans be classified as 'tool-making animals'?"

As I continued reading anything I could find on the nature of technology and communication media, I began to find some troubling ideas that made me wonder if technology was not all that it seemed. Very little of what I found considered these issues from a biblical or theological viewpoint, so I began to filter what I was reading through a biblical lens, documenting it in a blog entitled, "Don't Eat the Fruit."[1] This blog became the impetus for the book you hold in your hand today.

The blog's title is a reference to the Garden of Eden and the Jim Jones cult of the 1970s. In both cases, people consumed something they didn't fully understand, resulting in terrible consequences. In our modern world, we—like Adam, Eve, and Jim Jones's followers—often consume technology without being fully aware of the changes it can bring. This book is my attempt to grapple with those changes and understand how we can fulfill our role as God's image-bearers in a world very far removed from the garden.

As I did with the film projector so many years ago, I will use the following pages to dismantle the concept of technology, examine it carefully, and then put it back together again. I hope you enjoy this retelling of the story of technology in a way that honors God and the reason he put us here on earth.

1
PERSPECTIVE

Just down the street from my house, there is a little Indian market my family and I like to visit when we need to pick up a few items for dinner. On the short walk there we'll pass the neighbors from Korea who own a liquor store, the retired Germans with the meticulously kept lawn, a Chinese realtor who named both his dog and his daughter after himself, a tall Bolivian man who developed many of the algorithms for the 4G LTE networks that started coming online in 2010, the chief ice-cream scientist for an Italian gelato company, and an elderly black woman still displaced from Hurricane Katrina.

Some of these neighbors live in homes worth upwards of half a million dollars. They send their kids to expensive private schools, drive new luxury vehicles, and dress immaculately for every occasion. Just a few blocks away, however, another set of neighbors can barely afford their low-income government-subsidized housing. People from this group send their kids to public schools, travel by public transportation, and wear clothing from Goodwill.

Dotting the surrounding area are dozens of churches, mosques, temples, and synagogues, each serving the unique religious needs of our community. Scattered among these places of worship are dozens of restaurants serving every kind of cultural and ethnic food one can imagine. At the center of it all is Walmart, where you will find people wearing an equal number of burkas, Birkenstocks, and baggy jeans.

On the surface, then, my neighborhood would seem to be fairly diverse. We have different religions, genders, ages, occupations, food preferences, cultures, income levels, and native languages. And yet, this apparent diversity is actually a carefully crafted illusion.

If you look closely—brushing aside skin color, favorite religious texts, and socioeconomic status—you'll see that my neighbors and I have something in common that transcends all of our differences and orders nearly every part of our lives. It's obviously not our cultural heritage nor our common upbringing. It's not the place we live nor our hatred of the August heat in Texas.

The one thing that transcends all cultural, religious, and age boundaries, the one thing that is common among rich and poor and young and old, is the fact that we all share a lifestyle thoroughly saturated with technology.

A Completely Different World

At first glance it might seem that technology divides more than it unifies, for individuals and communities easily separate into high- and low-tech groups. I can tell the difference between the twelve-year-olds down the street who send hundreds of text messages a day and the little old ladies at the nearby nursing home who only use landlines. I know that the gigantic church a few miles away with HD video is far more technologically advanced than any of the smaller churches in the neighborhood. The houses in the new subdivision with solar panels, geothermal cooling, and computerized lighting are clearly much more advanced than the nearby HUD housing with incandescent lightbulbs and window A/C units.

However, only a narrow view of technology and culture leads to such a strict division between techie and technophobe.

If we broaden our perspective to consider the last several decades, our distinctions of techie versus non-techie vanish. Just a century ago, the idea of communicating electronically to anyone at any time would have seemed like magic. By the standards of 1900, the difference between communicating via landline or Skype would be meaningless, because a person from that era would not yet be accustomed to hearing disembodied voices from across the globe. Even the most educated and advanced individual of the 1840s could not see a distinction between the big-screen TVs of the 1980s (that took up an entire living room) and a modern 3D movie theater, because they lived in the time before photography was commonplace.

Almost all of the tools we use on a daily basis—cars, telephones, televisions, ballpoint pens, washing machines, lightbulbs, air-conditioning, and so on—were invented in the past 150 years, but these tools are so normal to us that it seems strange to call them *technology*. Computer scientist Alan Kay, inventor of the concept of computer windows, famously picked up on the way we understand technology by saying we tend to define it as "anything that was invented after you were born."[1]

Because of all this technology, our world has changed so drastically over the last fifty years that the biblical character Abraham of 2000 B.C. would probably have more in common with Abraham Lincoln of the early 1800s than Lincoln would have with us in the twenty-first century. Though Abraham and Abe are separated by some 3,800 years and several important technological advances, our sixteenth president would likely find our world more incomprehensible than that of ancient Ur.

Abraham's father raised cattle, and Mr. Lincoln planted pumpkins. By contrast, most of us spend the majority of our time indoors, working at desks with little knowledge of the natural world. Both men attended small religious gatherings with people they knew well from the surrounding area. We drive several miles to sit in huge auditoriums and watch screens with thousands of people, many of whom are strangers. Their water supply and bathrooms were outside; ours are inside. They lived in small, one-bedroom dwellings lit by candles; we live in comparatively enormous homes equipped with electricity, phone, cable, and Internet lines. They wrote letters and spoke in person; we write electronically and speak through devices. They weathered the seasons; we control the weather with air-conditioning.

We could go on making various comparisons, but the point is that our world is so uniformly technological that even in an ethnically and religiously diverse community like my neighborhood, the day-to-day activities of my neighbors probably have more in common with one another than with the founders of our country. Technology has become a kind of supracultural phenomenon that finds its way into every aspect of our diverse lives.

All but the poorest among us dwell in climate controlled buildings, wake up to digital alarm clocks, prepare meals with devices powered by a vast interconnected electrical grid, transport ourselves with vehicles fueled by internationally shipped petroleum, and ingest several thousand advertisements on billboards and screens scattered throughout our cities and homes. Not a single one of these devices or behaviors existed just over a century ago, and yet all of us treat them as if they were as normal as the water we drink or the air we breathe.

So why does any of this matter? If more advanced technology leads to things like increased quality of life and faster ways to spread the gospel, what could be the harm in any of it? Why do we need to pay close attention to the influence of technology? The story of a certain young pastor and yet another projector shows what can happen when we ignore technology.

The Youth Pastor and the Projector

After I graduated from college, I took a job as a youth pastor. One of my first requests was a video projector for our youth room. As a youth pastor at a *Bible* church, my job was to make sure the kids were firmly planted in the Scriptures. That meant that they needed to regularly encounter the words of the Bible with their own eyes. The only problem was that many of the kids didn't bring Bibles. I figured a projector would allow me to put the words of God on-screen so everyone could read together whether they brought a Bible or not. (And as a bonus, we could play video games on a gigantic screen and call it "ministry.")

Eventually, a generous church member donated a projector, and I immediately began using it during all my teaching. I made fantastic sermon outlines and highlighted important words in the text. I peppered my teaching with captivating stories and concluded them with hilarious punch lines. I taught verse-by-verse, but I also made the Scriptures relevant and applicable to the kids' lives. They seemed to eat it up, and at the risk of sounding haughty, I think I was a pretty good youth leader.

But then things started to go terribly wrong.

I started to notice that fewer and fewer kids were bringing their Bibles to church. And those who did bring them didn't open them when I was teaching. Perhaps I was not the model youth pastor I thought myself to be.

I tried saying, "Open your Bibles to . . ." more often, but that didn't seem to help—they just ignored me when I said it. I tried toning down my wit and charm and focusing more on the text of Scripture, but no matter how much I emphasized the Bible, the kids still wouldn't bring or open them. I even preached a few sermons on "Bibliology"—a pretty big term for thirteen-year-olds—but there was no change.

Finally, I pulled aside one of my students and said, "I talk to you guys all the time about how important the Bible is, but I notice you don't bring your Bible to church anymore. Why don't you think the Bible is important?"

She answered, "But I *do* think the Bible is important! I just like reading it on the screen with everybody else. Why would I bring a Bible if you project it on-screen?"

Of course, the conversation didn't happen exactly like that—it just sounds better that way for a book. But this situation opened my eyes to how the technologies that surround us can have an impact on something as intimate as how we encounter the Scriptures. I imagined that the projector would level the playing field and give everyone equal access to the Word of God. In my mind, a projector was a perfectly normal thing to bring into a church. All I was doing was taking the unchanging, eternal, inerrant Word of God and transferring it to a newer, better medium that had the power to reach more students. I never considered that the projector would completely transform the way my students encountered God's Word.

Years later, when I began to study the effects technology can have on people, I began to regret my ignorant perspective regarding technology. How could I have done so much damage to my kids without even knowing it? I shared what had happened with some friends, and many of them were horrified to learn that, as a result of my technological choices, suburban American kids—*gasp!*—weren't bringing their Bibles into church buildings. After all, what's a Bible church without Bibles?

However, as I contemplated this, I realized that my perspective was even more limited and myopic than I had first thought. Whereas I initially considered not bringing a Bible to church a tragedy, I soon realized that believers have only been doing this for the last few centuries. Until the printing press made Bibles inexpensive and available to everyone, individuals rarely owned their own copy of the Bible. Every single believer from Moses to Martin Luther—from 1500 B.C. to A.D. 1500—encountered God's Word by going to church and *listening* to it alongside others. They almost never had the chance to *read* the Bible for themselves. This meant that for nearly three thousand years, there was not a single believer in the one true God who ever had a "quiet time" as we know it today. Only rabbis and priests had access to handwritten copies of the Bible, but common people simply could not afford them. Gutenberg's printing press allowed families to purchase a copy of the Scriptures, but it was not until the twentieth century that it became common for individuals to own a personal copy of the Bible.

Looking back on what happened in my youth pastor days, the projector had actually allowed my kids to experience God's Word in a way much more similar to the pre-printing press era. My students had given up their individualized Bible with custom covers and specialized study notes and had begun reading the same words on the same screen together, as a group. By transitioning from print to projector, we had moved forward technologically and yet backward culturally.

It turns out that these kinds of cultural shifts have been well documented by historians of technology. Some even argue that the last five hundred years—from the time of the printing press to the time of projectors and the Internet—will be seen as an aberration in human history.[2] These five centuries will have been the only time in human history when printed text was the dominant form of communication. Today, with cell phones and online video chat, we are returning to a culture of spoken words rather than printed text, and yet those spoken words are not shared in person.

Our point here is not to argue that it is better to hear the Bible orally than it is to read it in print, or that reading on a screen with a group is better than either of those. Instead it is important to recognize how little attention we pay to the technologies we use to encounter the Word of God. While God's words are eternal and unchanging, the tools we use to access those words do change, and those changes in technology also bring subtle changes to the practice of worship. When we fail to recognize the impact of such technological change, we run the risk of allowing our tools to dictate our methods. Technology should not dictate our values or our methods. Rather, we must use technology *out of* our convictions and values.

The Myth of Technology

So why is it that we tend not to recognize the changes that technology brings? Why did I have so little awareness of how the printed Bible had shaped my expectation of church and how the projected Bible would re-shape it?

Neil Postman attempted to explain this by saying that over time, "technology tends to become mythic." By "myth" Postman wasn't referring to a legend or fantasy story. Instead, he used the word "myth" to describe the way of life that people think of as normal. In this sense, a myth is the story that develops over time about how the world works and what makes sense to a group of people. For example, most people know that leaders of the United States are chosen by voting. Before July 4, 1776, the idea of voting for leaders was new and radical, but over time voting has become a part of our shared "myth" about the way government is supposed to work.

When a new technology comes along, it too seems strange, out of place, and even magical at first. As sci-fi writer Arthur C. Clarke once quipped,

"Any sufficiently advanced technology is indistinguishable from magic."[3] Sitting in a coffee shop, the person with the brand-new laptop—a little slimmer and lighter than last year's model—stands out. However, as futurist Jamais Cascio writes, "as [technologies] move from the pages of a science fiction story to the pages of a catalog, something interesting happens: they lose their power to disturb. They're no longer the advance forces of the techpocalypse, they're the latest manifestation of the fashionable, the ubiquitous, and the banal. They're normal."[4]

Today nearly every adult has a mobile phone. Yet in the late 1990s, a mobile phone was considered a bit of an extravagance, only for very important businesspeople. Going back in time, the same could be said of portable music players (the first Sony Walkman was released in 1979), microwaves (1947), air-conditioning (1920s), and human flight (1903). Each technology was a revolution when it first arrived, but now they are all such a part of everyday life that it's difficult to imagine life without them.

The longer a particular practice or device has been around, the more solidly mythic it becomes in our culture. Eventually we stop thinking about why it was there in the first place, and over time we lose the ability—or desire—to question its presence. Those who might question a common technology—like email or mobile phones—might as well be crazy, or from another planet! It's like doubting that hot dogs should be eaten at sporting events or that Texans should have air-conditioning.

But when it comes to technology, each generation sees the issue from a slightly different perspective. Douglas Adams, author of *Hitchhiker's Guide to the Galaxy*, once grouped technology into three categories. First, "everything that's already in the world when you're born is just normal." Then, "anything that gets invented between then and before you turn thirty is incredibly exciting and creative and with any luck you can make a career out of it." Finally, "anything that gets invented after you're thirty is against the natural order of things and the beginning of the end of civilisation as we know it until it's been around for about ten years when it gradually turns out to be alright really."[5] In other words, each generation is equipped with a different myth concerning technology. The faster technology develops and the less perspective we have, the more stratified our myths become.

Shortsighted Critiques of Technology

These generational gaps mean that younger people often uncritically embrace any and all technology while older generations sometimes make shortsighted critiques of technology. Consider, for example, a recent *New York Times* article discussing how preteen children interact online and via text messaging. The author begins by describing how teens chat on Facebook late into the night, and her tone suggests that she disapproves of this new way of interacting through technology. She then laments, "Children used to actually talk to their friends. Those hours spent on the family princess phone or hanging out with pals in the neighborhood after school vanished long ago."[6]

The author obviously wants to contrast the technological communication her children engage in with the embodied, face-to-face encounters she remembers from her youth. But did you notice how she paired "hanging out with pals in the neighborhood after school" with "hours spent on the phone" as if both were equally nontechnological?

Chances are, the author was born after the telephone was invented and turned thirty sometime before texting and Facebook caught on. She goes on to wonder if texting is healthy and questions whether her children will be able to relate properly as they grow older. Yet, at the same time, spending "hours on the phone" seems like a perfectly normal—even *good*—way for kids to relate and communicate with one another. In fact, it appears that she sees no real difference between spending time together in person and talking on the phone. As long as she can hear a voice, it feels "real" to the author.

But I imagine that if we were to dig deeply into the *New York Times* archives, we might find a similar article written in the 1950s that would criticize "talking for hours on the phone." Just a generation ago, talking on the phone for hours would have seemed as foreign and unhealthy as the texting habits of today's children. If we were to dig even further back in the archives, a pattern would quickly emerge in which the older generation is worried about the technology of the new generation, while they are largely unaware of their own technological heritage. How can we question the next generation's technology if we don't even understand our own?

It turns out that the phenomenon of questioning new technology while clinging to older technology is not limited to *New York Times* authors and youth pastors like myself. It happens at all levels of society and in churches around the world.

Uncovering the Myth

What this tells us is that the way we talk about and understand technology is in some ways dictated by where we sit along the timeline of technological progress. Rather than taking our cues about technology from the Scriptures and the outline of God's plan for humanity, we seem to be locked in a cycle of questioning the really, really new but accepting the just barely old. We question the young for the blind acceptance of the latest gadgets, but we do so driving our computerized cars to and from church sipping on coffee grown on another continent.

Today's technology has the power to "heal the sick and make the blind see," and yet it also has the power to overwhelm us and distract us from what is truly important. When technology has distracted us to the point that we no longer examine it, it gains the greatest opportunity to enslave us.

To avoid this cycle, we'll need to start from the beginning and explore how the Scriptures treat technology. In the coming chapters, we will follow the outline of the biblical story beginning with creation and continuing to the fall to redemption and finally to restoration. Like a good seminary graduate, I've relabeled the first two chapters of the story so that all four start with the letter "R": Reflection, Rebellion, Redemption, and Restoration.

As we discover the role of technology in each section of the biblical story, it will lead us to a follow-up question that will help us better understand technology. In chapter 3, we will delve into the creation where God gives humanity the role of reflecting his image and charges them with cultivating and keeping the garden. In the following chapter, we will explore the unique role of technology among the things humans create. Then in chapter 5, we will look at Adam and Eve's rebellion (the fall) and the subsequent evil uses of technology that find their origin in Cain and his family. This will lead us to explore a more fully developed philosophical approach to technology in chapter 6. In chapter 7, we will begin exploring the various mediums[7] through which God accomplishes his plan of redemption, and in chapter 8 we will see how those mediums operate within a culture and how they shape individuals. In chapter 9, we will complete the biblical story by looking at what God will do when he restores the earth. Chapter 10 will pick up where the biblical story left off, examining how the world of technology has continued to develop into a kind of religion unto itself. Finally, in chapter 11 we will look at the digital revolution and use what we've learned to help us understand, and live faithfully in, our current age.

At one end of this story is a pristine garden prepared by God for humankind to develop and transform. At the other end is a glorious, heavenly city full of human creations, art, and technology. At the center is our Savior Jesus Christ crucified on a cross, the most horrific of all technological distortions, built by transforming a tree from the natural world into a tool of death. Yet in his resurrection, Christ redeemed even that tool, transforming it into the symbol of our faith that eternally portrays his power over death and sin.

In the time between the garden and the city, between Christ's first and second coming (when he will complete his work of redemption and restoration), we must work diligently to understand how to live faithfully in this technology-saturated world. To help us better understand our world, we will combine what we find in the Scriptures with insights from some of the best thinkers on technology, theology, and culture. We can't give adequate attention to heavyweights like Heidegger,[8] but his work will inform us as we retell the biblical story. We will also limit our discussion to "everyday" kinds of technology, meaning that we won't attempt to address important societal issues like health care, nuclear weapons, or biotechnology.[9]

Discerning Technology

It would be exceedingly convenient if we could simply label every technology as either "good" (use it as much as you want) or "bad" (never, ever use it). But Arthur Boers posits that technology is more like the yellow light on a traffic signal.[10] Unlike green, which always means "go," or red, which always means "stop," the yellow light is a call for a discerning look at the entire situation.

A surprisingly helpful example of this kind of technological discernment can be found in an obscure passage in one of John's letters. In 2 John 12, the apostle wrote:

> Though I have much to write to you, I would rather not use paper and ink. Instead I hope to come to you and talk face to face, so that our joy may be complete.

In 3 John 12–13, he repeated the same idea:

> I had much to write to you, but I would rather not write with pen and ink. I hope to see you soon, and we will talk face to face.

In John's day, "pen and ink" was the communication tool he was tasked with evaluating, and though it might seem low tech to us today, it too had its detractors.

A few hundred years before John wrote his letters, the Greek philosopher Socrates expressed concern about the technology of writing. He believed that learning in dialogue was the key to helping people grow in wisdom, and he worried that writing would make people knowledgeable, but it would fail to make them wise. Socrates was so worried about the damage that writing could cause that he never wrote any of his own ideas down.[11]

In his letters, John seems to be aware of the drawbacks that writing, as a technology, brings. In fact, he says that he would prefer not to use it for communication because he valued embodied, face-to-face reality more than the disembodied words of a letter. He goes so far as to say that it is only in face-to-face conversation that he finds fullness of joy.

While upholding the value of embodied reality over technology, John still saw the value in communicating through the medium of writing. In this case, it was impossible for him to be present with his audience. And in the wisdom and leading of the Holy Spirit, John's writings need to be preserved for the rest of the church. So fully aware of the strengths and weaknesses of the new technology of writing, John makes a calculated choice to use a disembodied form of communication in service of the embodied life of the church, and in doing so he honors our Lord and builds up his Body.

My hope is that in the coming chapters we can learn to do the same with our technology.

2

IMAGINATION

Of all of my parents' friends, my favorite was a couple from Mississippi who gave us a huge, wooden fort. The fort was over twenty feet tall, with a ladder reaching up into the main platform and a pole sliding back down for quick escapes. For my brothers and me, the fort was the perfect opportunity for our young imaginations to run wild. That fort transformed us into pirates at sea, cowboys warding off outlaws, and knights storming the castle.

It's commonly held that adults have lost the propensity for imaginative play. While kids have the ability to look past the world as it is and see the world as it could be, adults are only able to see the real world. A select few storytellers can create new worlds with their pens and keyboards, but most of us, we are told, can no longer imagine such places for ourselves.

Yet when it comes to using technology, the ability to imagine and tell stories is awakened even in adults. In fact, whenever we use a tool—whether it be a shovel or a cell phone—three powerful stories unfold.

The First Story

The first story tells how humans shape the world using tools. This larger story begins with the smaller stories we tell ourselves when we see a new tool. As we imagine ourselves using it, we see in our mind's eye all the great new things we can accomplish with the device. Whether we come across a faster computer, an egg white separator, or a space shuttle, our minds attempt to understand the tool by imagining what it would be like to use it.

Historian of technology David Nye writes, "Composing a narrative and using a tool . . . . Each requires the imagination of altered circumstances. . . . In each case, one imagines how present circumstances might be made different."[1] Just as storytellers imagine new worlds for their books and movies, we too envision an alternate reality when we imagine how we'll use a tool. We see the world as it is, and then through the tool we see the world as it could be.

Like little boys making their hands into the shapes of pistols and imagining what the world would be like as daring and important cowboys, adults imagine how the world might be better, faster, or cleaner if only we had that robotic vacuum cleaner, the four-wheel-drive vehicle, or a high-resolution mobile phone. The mind of a child envisions a world of adventure and purpose while the mind of an adult longs for a world of comfort, ease, and power.

Not all of us, however, imagine the story the same way. Some look at new gadgets and think, "Wow, that would make my life so much easier." Others have the opposite reaction: "That's ridiculous," they say. "I would never need that thing." However, even though the reactions are polar opposites, both engage in the act of imagining what it would be like to use the tool, and both base their conclusions about the tool on how the story ends.

Though we might not realize it, we compose these mininarratives whenever we encounter even the simplest gadget. If we happen to see a shovel, our minds can easily imagine the act of digging a hole, visualizing how the ground will look after we're finished. This small effort of the imagination has a clear movement from beginning (the world before the shovel) to middle (the act of digging) to end (the world with a new hole)—the basic arc of any story. It might not be a long story, or a particularly interesting one, but it's still a story; and when it's over, the world will be a different place. After all, there is now a hole in the ground.

But the stories we tell ourselves about tools have an important difference from the stories we read in books. As we read a story in a book, we are transported to an alternate world that the author has crafted from carefully chosen words. For a little while we inhabit that world and are possibly even transformed by it. Eventually, however, we must return to the real world; and we realize that those places and those people don't really exist.

Yet when we use technology, we are no longer constructing a fictional world using words. Instead, we are reconstructing the actual world using tools. Unlike tales of goblins or love at first sight, the stories we tell ourselves about technology can become everyday realities. If we imagine a world with a hole, a shovel can create that world for us. And if we imagine a world free from headaches, medicine can make that a reality.

Technology, then, is the bridge from this world to the imagined one. Storybooks give us a glimpse into an alternate world, but technology allows us to actually live in an alternate world. From Adam's invention of clothing to Edison's invention of the lightbulb, technology is the means by which we transport ourselves to the better worlds we are constantly imagining. The more powerful the tool, the more fully our visions can be realized. When we stumble into a problem we want to solve, we instinctively search for a tool that can help us get from the world with the problem to a world where the problem is solved.

If you're not yet convinced of the link between tools and our love of stories, you need only to observe any advertisement in print, TV, or on the Internet. In thirty seconds or less, advertisements tap into the basic movement from our present circumstances to a newer, better world. First, the commercial will call attention to a problem in our lives. Then it will promise a brighter, cleaner, and faster world made possible by the product on-screen. In fact, every single commercial we watch or hear has the basic plot structure of beginning (our current limited existence), middle (acquiring a shiny new tool), and end (a better world only available to those with the tool).

Commercials for fast cars promise to transport the buyer to a thrilling world of speed and social status. Billboards for new shaving products promise the buyer a world free from the nicks and cuts offered by competitors. Banner ads for new electronic gadgets guarantee the buyer more free time, productivity, and fun. Mr. Clean showcases homes unsoiled and minty-fresh, and celebrities promise whatever they are selling will make us as beautiful and successful as they are.

A perfect example of how advertising attempts to capitalize on the desire for new tools comes from a 2010 Sprint advertisement that asked, "What will you do with EVO, the first 4G phone?" Notice that Sprint's marketing department is inviting the viewer to imagine life with the device. Sprint knows that triggering the constant creative yearning for a better world can convince the viewer that the new Sprint phone is the answer. And a convinced viewer will buy whatever is offered.

The allure of technology, then, is a promise that the right tools will bring about a better world. We continually tell ourselves that with technology we can take this broken world and mold it into the better one that we all desire. The transforming role of technology is evidenced in the way many scholars define technology. For example, Dutch engineering professor and theologian Egbert Schuurman writes, "We can say that we are talking about technology when we use tools to shape nature in the service of human ends."[2] David Mindell sees technology as the "constellation of tools, machinery, systems, and techniques that manipulate the natural world for human ends."[3]

Technology, then, is the means by which we transform the world as it is into the world that we desire. What we often fail to notice is that it is not only the world that gets transformed by technology. We, too, are transformed.

The Second Story

If the first story of technology is how we humans shape the world using tools, the second story is how those tools in turn shape us.

To see how this happens, let's again use the example of our trusty shovel. Imagine for a moment that we see an advertisement telling us how exciting our world could be with several holes in the ground. The advertisement convinces us that a shovel is the means by which we can get to the wonderful world of holes, and so we purchase the shovel and begin digging. After some time we put the shovel down, wipe our brow, and survey the work we have done. Proudly, we see the world is quite different than it was a few hours ago. We, dear friends, are now standing on holey ground.

But if we stop for a moment more and look down, turning our palms toward our eyes, we'll see that our hands, too, have been changed by the shovel. They will be rubbed raw, exposing the first sign of the blisters that are sure to develop while we sleep.[4]

Over time, as we dig hole after hole, reshaping the world as we see fit, our hands, arms, and backs will be changed as well. Those blisters will turn into calluses, and our once weak arms will grow stronger and more muscular. Our minds too will develop a sense of the land and how best to approach it. When the job is completed, the tool will have transformed both the creator and the creation. Indeed as John Culkin, a student of Marshall McLuhan, wrote, "We shape our tools and thereafter our tools shape us."[5]

In this sense, technology sits between us and the world, changing and molding both at once. The world feels the spade, but we feel the handle. We use the tool to dig at the ground, but in another sense the ground uses the tool to chafe at our hands. The shovel connects us to the earth, but it also functions to insulate us from directly touching the soil. Our primary connection then is with the tool, not the creation itself, giving the tool the opportunity to simultaneously shape both the world and its user.

But notice that the transformation technology brings happens regardless of *why* a person uses a tool. One person might use a shovel to break ground on a new orphanage, while another might use it to conceal stolen goods. Clearly, one is morally superior to the other, but the moral intent does not change the fact that both the righteous and the wicked end up with blisters and aching backs. The moral purpose of digging does not change the way that the act of using a shovel transforms a person.

Though most of us don't approach technology in this way, we actually do this purposefully all the time: we regularly use tools expressly designed to transform our bodies. Treadmills, for example, are engineered to help us become more physically fit. The more we use a treadmill, the longer and leaner our leg muscles become, and the stronger and more powerful our hearts grow. In a sense, a treadmill transports us to a world where we can stay physically fit without ever leaving a building.

Of course, if we choose a different tool of physical transformation, such as a leg press, our legs will take on a different shape. The more leg presses we do, the larger and stronger our quadriceps will become. Over time we can build up incredible leg strength and muscle mass, transforming our ability as well as our appearance.

It is important to recognize that the more we master these two tools—the treadmill and the leg press—the further they take us in one direction, but not the other. Marathon runners usually cannot lift six hundred pounds with their legs, and those that can perform such a feat usually cannot run marathons. One tool transforms us in one area, while a different tool changes us into something else. This is certainly a rather extreme example, but it highlights how important it is to be aware of the ways in which our tools shape us.

And while our trusty shovel molds us physically, technology can shape us in other ways as well. From radio to television to the Internet, scientists and cultural critics have long contended that our communication and information technologies influence the way we think in the same way that shoes affect the way we run. Most recently, Nicholas Carr argues in his book *The Shallows*[6] that our brains work just like our muscles; when we perform a mental task repeatedly, our neural pathways rewire themselves to become better at that task.

For example, people who spend long hours reading books with complex ideas tend to become good at that activity. Likewise, people who spend their days consuming small pieces of information such as text messages or status updates tend to have minds particularly suited to performing that task. But just as it is difficult to master both running long distances and lifting heavy weights with our legs, these two mental tasks are mutually exclusive to a

degree. Those who have developed the ability to consume complex arguments in books tend to feel overwhelmed by the rush of data online, while
those who do most of their reading online and on small mobile screens tend
to lose concentration when they attempt to focus on a single idea for long
periods of time. For example, this book is around sixty thousand words,
meaning an average reader should be able to finish it in around five hours.
However, those that have developed the skill of reading online may find it
difficult to read a book for that duration.

Again, as with the blisters and calluses from a shovel, these mental trans-
formations happen without reference to morality. Whether a person spends
long periods of time reading Christian apologetics or spends that time
reading atheist literature, the reader will increase the ability to understand
complex arguments. And whether a person reads thousands of tweets from
Ashton Kutcher and Britney Spears or thousands of tweets from John Piper
and a C. S. Lewis robot, the skill of consuming massive amounts of small
information bites will increase.

In each of these cases, the effect of technology on the brain and body
happen irrespective of the content. Of course, the content we consume is
important, but often we focus so much on the content that we miss the
importance of the medium through which we consume it. In fact, sometimes the effects of a medium are more important than any content trans-
mitted through that medium.

Marshall McLuhan coined the now famous phrase, "The medium is the
message," to describe this phenomenon, saying, "This is merely to say that
the personal and social consequences of any medium—that is, of any extension of ourselves—result from the new scale that is introduced into our
affairs by each extension of ourselves or by any new technology."[7]

What he meant was that the transformative effect of a technology is so
powerful that it often overshadows what we say or do with that medium.
In the exercise examples above, the treadmill is the medium and its transformative message is increasing our ability to run. With the medium of
Twitter, the message is increasing our ability to consume short, disconnected sentences.

McLuhan's main interest was not the blisters individuals receive from the shovel but rather the social and cultural transformation that happens in a group of people who have shovels. When we use tools to transform the world into the one we imagine, everyone around us is forced to respond and adapt to those changes. For example, when music moved from CDs to digital downloads, we were transported to a world where music was easier to find and purchase. But this technological change also changed the relationships between bands, labels, producers, and consumers. It doesn't matter if we buy classical music, Christian music, or music with explicit lyrics, the medium of digital downloads sends a message to the music industry.

This happens because technology is not only situated between us and the world but also between one human and another. Right now, this book functions as an interface between you and me. Through the technologies of language, writing, paper, ink, and e-books, you have access to the thoughts I've written. Just as a shovel is an interface between the builder and the world, this book is a channel between writer and reader. In one sense, the book connects two minds previously disconnected. And yet, at the same time it connects, the book also forms a wedge between two people. When one person is reading another's thoughts, those two people cannot be fully present to one other. Just as a builder accesses the dirt through the medium of the shovel, we access the minds of others through our various communication mediums. Builders don't have direct access to dirt, and you and I don't have direct access to one another.

And so it is with cell phones, email, video chat, and all of the communication tools we use today. They both connect us and put something between us. Psalm 1 tell us that we are molded and shaped by the company we keep, but when we connect with people through technology, the medium becomes part of the equation in how that molding and shaping takes place.

Technology has the power to transform the world into the one we imagine, but it also has the power to transform our bodies, our mental capabilities, and our relational worlds. But there is a third, even more powerful story that technology has to tell.

The Third Story

The third and final story we tell with technology happens when all that transforming we do to the world and ourselves finds its way into our souls. We know that shovels transform the earth and reshape our hands, but—taking a step back—we must wonder why humans dig at all. Computers help us compute things, but what is the big question we are trying to answer? Cars take us from here to there, but where exactly are we going? In other words, why are we doing all of this technology?

One obvious answer might be that we are trying to reduce suffering in the world, and thankfully technology has in fact accomplished that to some degree. In 1850, the average life expectancy of someone living in North America or Europe was around thirty-eight years.[8] But today, the average life expectancy is well over seventy years. That means that in less than two centuries, technology advanced to a point where it doubled the length of our lives. Much of this increase is due to advances in obstetrics, which led to a drop in the infant mortality rate from three hundred deaths per a thousand births in 1850 to just twenty deaths per a thousand births in 2000.[9] My personal gratitude for such advances increased dramatically in the moments when I watched helplessly as a surgeon wheeled my wife into an operating room with our first child trapped in her birth canal, his body turned upside down and his left ear smashed against his shoulder. As little as fifty years ago, I might have experienced the pain and anguish of losing both a cherished wife and a precious child. Thankfully, however, I was rescued from living that story and taken to a world where on a daily basis I experience the joy, laughter, and beauty of marriage and parenthood.

Certainly, then, I would consider medical technology to be a good and even redemptive thing, and I see this world as better and more advanced than the one of the 1900s. But what do I really mean when I say, "more advanced"? What are we advancing toward? Where are we going? One day, both my wife and my children will die, as will I. Would a world with technology that allowed us to live indefinitely—free from disease and even death—be a "better" world than this one?

How we answer these kinds of questions leads us to one of two ways of understanding technology and describing life. In one story, there is a God who is moving humanity along a timeline. He has a purpose and a plan, and there is an end point toward which he is moving all of history. Technology plays a role in this story, but it is a subservient role, not an ultimate one. The only true salvation offered to humanity comes from God himself, through his Son Jesus Christ.

In the other story, there is no God. There is only the advancement of life itself from simple to more complex. In the first few billion years, this advancement was biological in nature, but now the primary means of progressing and advancing life is technological. If there is any salvation or any hope for the future, it will come through the advancement of technology. In biological terms humanity is known as *homo sapiens* ("knowing man" or "wise man"), but our true nature is that of *homo faber* ("making man" or "skilled man") because we advance our kind through the things we make. A recent article on prehistoric technology begins with, "Long before the BlackBerry, primates were obsessed with gadgets,"[10] implying that we are just the next stage in a long line of ever-evolving, tool-using animals with no design or purpose other than survival. Our ultimate destiny, the posthumanists contend, is to transcend our weak biological bodies and be born again into eternal machines.

Obviously, these two stories are at odds. In one story, God is our savior, while in the other, technology is what saves. In one story, God is the source of our resurrection and eternal life; in the other, technology becomes our god who enables our ascension into eternal life. And although the idea that technology can save us has become increasingly popular in the past few centuries, the origin of that story actually began long ago. From the moment Adam and Eve first sinned, and continuing with the life of their son Cain, technology has played a powerful role in the lives and identity of those who reject God. What we see today is the continuation of an unbroken line of humanity that consciously or unconsciously views technology as a god and savior. Today, David Hopper asks, "Has not technology come to embody our chief values—the things we want most out of life?"[11]

But what about us, the people of God? How are we to view technology? If God is our savior and he wins in the end, does technology even matter? Obviously, we should use technology for good and not for evil, but does anything more need to be said? If it is true that technology has the capacity to shape the world that God made, as well as shape our bodies, minds, and souls, then it seems we should care deeply about our tools. Moreover, if technology plays some role in the story of God redeeming his people, we should care all the more. So let us now turn to the Scriptures and discover where technology began.

REFLECTION

If you've ever tried to learn any computer programming, you might recognize the words "Hello World." That's because whenever a new programming language is created, the first thing its creator does is explain to everyone else how to write a simple program that makes the words "Hello World" appear on-screen. For example, in the famous programming language C, the code looks something like this:

```
main() {
  printf("hello world");
}
```

And in PHP, the language used to make popular websites like Facebook and Wordpress, it looks like this:

```php
<?php

  echo "Hello World";

?>
```

Even if you've never seen the code for a computer program before, these examples should be at least partially readable to you. You can spot the words "Hello World," and you might have guessed that everything else around it tells the computer to send those words to the screen. One of the things that has always fascinated me about programming is that it allows us to create working tools using nothing but words. We don't need any raw materials or physical strength, just pure creativity.

Of course, our task in this book is not to learn about programming but to understand something about what the Scriptures say about technology. And when we open up to the first pages of the Bible, we find God doing a kind of programming of his own. He, too, is not dependent on raw materials but can instead create by the power of his word. Yet unlike our dependence on computers or electricity, God really can create something from nothing.

In this and the coming chapters, we will reexamine familiar biblical stories and look for clues about how we should approach technology. From the outset, I want to make it clear that we won't take the time to acknowledge every nuance or important theological detail in the text. Neither will we attempt to answer questions about the relationship of science and history to the biblical stories. Instead we will simply assume that the Scriptures are trustworthy, and that they have much to tell us . . . including some things about technology.

How We're Programmed

In the opening chapter of Genesis, as God is creating the universe, he gives each of his creations a purpose and a function. To the stars he gives the job of separating day and night and marking out the seasons. To the plants he gives the job of sprouting fruit and seed. To the fish—what the Hebrew literally calls "the swimming things"—God says simply, "Swim." And to the birds—literally "the flying things"—he says, "Fly." During those first six days, every plant and animal received a place and a function within God's world. What they are made to *do*—shining, sprouting, swimming, and flying—in part defines what they *are*.

What, then, are human beings? If all the other creatures are defined by what they do, what is the thing that we humans *do* that makes us human? In other words, how did God program us?

Later on the sixth day, God answered this question by defining humanity not as creatures that sprout, swim, or fly but by saying, "Let us make man in our image" (Gen. 1:26). This means that our job, and the essence of what it is to be human, is to reflect God's image to the rest of creation. Of course many theologians have worn out their keyboards trying to demystify what it means to reflect God's image, but we can expound using four categories.

First, humans display God's ability to think rationally. Although some animals display a form of intelligence, humans are clearly distinct from the rest of the created order. Secondly, many thinkers have noticed the plural language referring to God ("let *us*") and proposed that humans reflect God's relationality. In our sin we attempt to live independent of our need for God and others, but God originally designed humans to function in a deeply interdependent way that reflects the tri-personhood of God. Thirdly, just as God is the ruler over the entire universe and all created things, his image-bearers are to rule over this tiny little planet. In Genesis 1 God commanded Adam (and successive humanity) to "have dominion" and "subdue the earth."

These three facets of humanity—our rational thinking, our relational nature, and our call to subdue the earth—are all undoubtedly reflections of God's nature. But we discover a final category as we move into Genesis 2, and it is this one that needs a bit more explanation.

Whereas Genesis 1 offers a panoramic view of the entire universe, Genesis 2 zooms in on God's design and production of humanity. Unlike the lush, full world of Genesis 1, chapter 2 begins with a barren, lifeless landscape where "no plant of the field had yet sprouted" (Gen. 2:5). Part of the reason for this was that "God had not caused it to rain," but the other issue was that "there was no man to work the ground." In Hebrew, there's a little wordplay going on because the word for ground (*adama*) sounds like the word for man (*adam*). Literally it reads, "there was no *adam* for the *adama*." Then God responds by picking up some of the dust from the dry, barren landscape and sculpting that dust into the first human being.

But God's image-bearer wasn't meant to live in an arid wasteland, and so before God does anything with Adam, he first plants the Garden of Eden and fills it with tall trees, ripe fruit, and flowing rivers. Once the garden is prepared, God gently sets Adam down within and gives him a simple job: "cultivate it and keep it" (Gen. 2:15 NASB). The air has flying things that fly, the sea has swimming things that swim, and now, finally, the *adama* has *Adam* to cultivate it. If the fish were programmed to swim and the birds were programmed to fly, then humans were programmed to cultivate the garden.

This tells us something important about both human nature and the garden. It means that God designed the garden—even before the fall, sin, and death—in such a way that it needed to be worked on. It's not that there was anything *wrong* with the garden, it's just that God didn't intend for it to stay the way that it was. Instead, God wanted Adam to "cultivate" or "till" or "work" what he found in the garden and make something new out of it. God created the garden not as an end point but as a starting place. Adam's job was to take the raw materials of the earth—from the wood of the trees, to the rocks on the ground, to the metal buried deep within the earth—and create new things from them. In a sense, Adam was to take the "natural" world (what God made) and fashion it into something else—something not entirely "natural"—but sanctioned by God.

Of course, God did put some limits on Adam. As we all know, God warned Adam not to eat from the Tree of the Knowledge of Good and Evil. But God also put limits on Adam's creative powers. The command to "cultivate the garden" was coupled with the command to "keep the garden." That word *keep* can also mean "guard" or "watch over," and it conveys the idea that Adam was not only to shape the garden but to maintain something of its original form. He was not to overcultivate it or use its raw materials in a way that would unnecessarily harm it or God's creatures. This is, of course, easier said than done especially in the unfortunate circumstance we find ourselves in today where "creation care" and "the environment" have become highly politicized. Nevertheless, it seems that God is asking us to strike a careful balance between "natural" and "unnatural," between the acts of cultivating and keeping.

Within these limits, Adam could do whatever he wanted in the garden, rearranging and creating from it as he saw fit. He could add a row of stones around trees he liked or make a bridge over one of the rivers. He could build a storage shed out of shells or collect seeds and plant them in rows. Whatever he chose to do, he would be taking what God had made and remaking it into a creation of his own. And in doing so, Adam would be reflecting the creativity of his Creator (who, at this point in the story, had done little but create).

The final aspect of our role as God's image-bearers, then, is our ability to create. When we cultivate the garden, that is, when we make things from what God has made, we are reflecting the image of God.

But something else important happens when we create. By choosing to put rocks around one set of trees and not another, Adam would be making a decision about what was important to him. By adding a bridge over this part of that river, Adam would be making a choice about the way he thought things should work. With each creative act, he would be making decisions about what matters and how things should be done. As he modeled behaviors to Eve and their children—and then Adam's children in turn modeled those same behaviors to their children—Adam's choices would form the basis of what these people considered important and meaningful.

Theologian Stanley Grenz groups the things we create into four broad categories: things, images, rituals, and language.[1] A *thing* is simply any physical object that people create, from a bridge over a river to the utensils with which we eat. *Images*, though objects also, are designed to represent something else, like a company logo, a symbol on a traffic sign, or the cross that represents our faith. *Rituals* are what we do with those things and images, including the time of year when we plant vegetables, how we wake up in the morning, how we brush our teeth, and the way we make coffee. Finally, *language* is the tool we use to share the meaning of these objects, images, and rituals.

As we create and use things, images, rituals, and language with others, we are sharing not only those items but also what they mean to us. The word we use to summarize this transfer of meaning is *culture*. In fact, these passages in Genesis 1 and 2 have sometimes been called the "culture mandate" because theologians find in it the command and responsibility for humans to create culture.

Now, there are probably as many definitions and views of culture as there were trees in the garden—and the word *culture* brings with it things like "culture wars," "high culture" versus "low culture," and the debate over "Christ and culture"—but we are going to use the word *culture* in a very simple way. My good friend Professor Barry Jones would say that the sharing of things, images, rituals, and language mediates three things to us: identity, meaning, and values. Theologian Emil Brunner captured this idea when he wrote that culture is the "materialization of meaning,"[2] but I did not fully understand what he meant until I experienced it firsthand.

An Altar in the Garden

A few years after I graduated from college, I started to wonder how my mom managed to raise four great kids as a single parent. One day she answered my question by taking me on a walk at a nearby park we used to visit when I was growing up. As we were walking along, my mom stopped for a moment to point out a small pile of rocks a few yards off the main pathway.

The pile was small enough that I hadn't noticed it at first, but once she pointed to it, I could see that it was human-made. The rocks obviously couldn't have gotten that way themselves—someone had collected and arranged them. After looking at them for a minute, I asked her, "What is it?"

My mom started to talk about how hard it was on her when my dad left. He gave her a lot of financial support and came to see us regularly, but she still felt crushed by the weight of raising us alone. Most of the time, the only thing she felt strong enough to do was pray for us. So every day while we were off at school, she would walk out to this spot and spend a few hours begging God to protect us. As God answered her prayers, she found some nearby rocks and built this little altar to mark the place where God had been faithful to our family.

As she told her story, that ordinary pile of rocks turned into something of enormous meaning to me. My mother had made this little place more important than the places in front of us and the places behind us. God had done something meaningful for my family, and my mother materialized that meaning into a tangible, visible, material form. She did this by taking what God had made—a few simple rocks—and remaking it into something that reflected the creativity and goodness of God.

Growing up, my mom never talked about her little altar, but when she finally told me about it, it changed me. I could never again see myself as a person whom God had forgotten. My identity was altered such that I now see myself as a person who was an answer to prayer. Those stones said I would not be who I was if God had not acted.

Using Grenz's terminology, my mom's altar was a "thing" around which she had built a "ritual" of consistent prayer for her children. When my mother shared her altar with me, it was deeply meaningful to me, and it mediated the value of a life of prayerfulness as well as a new sense of identity.

While the example of my mom's altar might seem extraordinary, this kind of mediation of values happens anytime we create—and even when we rearrange—everyday things. For example, imagine that you walked into a roomful of twenty chairs. If those chairs were arranged in four rows of five with a podium up front, you would immediately know this was some kind of classroom with a clear authority figure. But if those same chairs were arranged in a circle, you would tend to interpret it as a group-oriented setting where everyone is equal. The "culture" of the room would be determined by both the presence of chairs and the arrangement of them. Every day we participate in dozens of these little cultures. Our homes, offices, churches, cities, and countries each encompass a unique set of things, images, rituals, and language that forms its identity and communicates meaning and value.

Technology Culture

So what does all this talk of culture and meaning have to do with technology? Underneath those things, images, rituals, and language are the tools we use to create them. Andy Crouch recently wrote that culture is simply "what we make of the world,"[3] and we might say that technology is "how" we make what we are making. But tools are also themselves "cultural goods," and as we discussed in the previous chapter, they not only help us cultivate the garden, they also work to cultivate us. We use tools to create cultural goods, yet because those tools are themselves elements of culture, they too mediate a set of values, meaning, and identity back to us.

If you ask the average person, "What is the meaning of your cell phone and what sense of identity and values does it mediate to you?" you might be answered by a confused look. But if you ask, "How would you *feel* if you lost your cell phone?" the immediacy of the answer would betray deep beliefs about what it means to be connected. It may be that the cell phone is not just a tool but an integral part of the person's identity, who they define themselves to be.

We will spend much of the next chapter more carefully distinguishing technology from other cultural goods, but before we close this chapter, we should address one final question about creating and culture. We don't live in the Garden of Eden, and the things, images, and rituals of today's cultures and subcultures don't always reflect the values of our Creator. The wickedness of much of today's culture has led some to believe that culture is synonymous with worldliness. Therefore it's hard to believe that culture and technology actually existed in the garden.

Yet the word translated *cultivate* in Genesis 2 is elsewhere translated *till*, an action that assumes the use of tools. This seems to indicate that using tools was a part of God's design for humanity even before the fall. But even more importantly, if we look carefully at Genesis 2, we'll see that the first elements of culture—and the first tools that both shaped the world and the humans who used them—were created *in the garden*.

The First Technology

If you ask a cultural anthropologist or evolutionary biologist to identify the most important tool developed by early humans, they will invariably say it was language. Even monkeys use stone tools, but it was language that allowed humans to build and share knowledge. Interestingly, Genesis seems to agree with this line of thinking.

After God put Adam in the garden to "cultivate and keep it," he gave Adam his first creative task. As God created the animals, he "brought them to the man to see what he would call them. And whatever the man called every living creature, that was its name." Genesis goes on to say that, "The man gave names to all livestock and to the birds of the heavens and to every beast of the field" (Gen. 2:20).

From the way this section of Scripture ends, we surmise that this exercise was in part designed to show Adam that none of the animals could serve as a "suitable helper" for him. But the text also tells us that God had a second purpose in mind. Apparently God wanted "to see what he [Adam] would call them" (Gen. 2:19). In other words, he wanted to watch as Adam *created* language.

There in the garden, as he created words and names that didn't exist before, Adam started reflecting the image of God. These words would serve as the lens through which Eve and their children would see those creatures.

Now we don't ordinarily think of language as a technology, but language is very much a tool. Not only is it a tool, but it is a tool we use to inform and categorize the way we see the world. Embedded in our language lies our values and identity.

When my son was learning his first words, my wife and I loved to see what he called things. The first animal name he learned was "duck," and since that was the only word he knew, he called everything "duck"... dogs, cats, birds, elephants, and every other living creature. He was constantly pointing to anything that moved and shouting, "DUCK!" Thankfully, he soon started learning additional categories like fish and cat and bird, and the more words he learned, the more he could communicate with us. Later he began learning his colors, and I loved watching his little face as he studied an object, categorized it, and then blurted out a new word. Where he used to just see a collection of undifferentiated objects, he could now organize that visual space using the colors and names we had given him. But we don't just use language to categorize things; we also use language to represent our values. For example, the word *bachelor* describes a man whom our culture believes is old enough to have married but who has not done so. The existence of the word *bachelor* shows that English-speaking cultures value marrying at a certain age.

As we teach my son the English language, we are introducing him to our culture and giving him the tool set through which he will see the world. But if we were not English speakers and we taught him a different language, then he would see the world in a slightly different way. Language, like all of our tools, operates as a filter between us and the world. The language that we speak and through which we think tints what we see in the world.

For example, English words generally don't have gender, but most German and Spanish nouns are categorized as masculine, feminine, or neuter. This is important because some words like *bridge* are feminine in German, but masculine in Spanish. Other words like *key* are the opposite—masculine in German, but feminine in Spanish. When you learn these languages, teachers usually say that the gender doesn't actually matter, but a recent study proved otherwise. It showed that German speakers tended to describe bridges in feminine terms like "elegant" and "peaceful," while native Spanish speakers used words like "towering," "strong," and "dangerous." When it came to keys, they did just the opposite. The Germans felt that keys were "hard," "heavy," and "jagged," while their Spanish friends spoke in terms like "intricate," "little," and "lovely."[4]

That study is evidence that language works like a pair of sunglasses; it colors the way we see everything, from bridges to keys to other people. The authors of the same study also found a small Aboriginal community whose language lacks directional words such as "behind" and "in front of." Instead, to identify an object, members of the community use cardinal directions like "the mountain to the north" or "the man to the west of you." They might even say, "There's an ant on your southwest leg." This kind of language requires them to stay oriented in space at all times in order to function. Unlike those of us who see objects in the world in relationship to other objects, their language identifies the object relative to the earth itself. This is valuable for a culture who spends most of its time outdoors. But language of this nature has no value for those who live mostly indoors. In other words, the value system of this Aboriginal dialect would conflict with the value system embedded in the English language.

Cultures develop and modify language so that it reflects the culture's needs, that is, what they want from the world. Today this is evident in the adolescent culture with teenagers who do much of their communication via text messaging. Teenagers are constantly introducing new abbreviations, shortcuts, and combinations of characters that help them transfer their values back and forth among themselves. As they change their language, though, they are also creating a distinct culture. Those who do not understand these texting conventions may not be a part of their culture. This means that kids and parents living in the same household can be a part of different cultures. This fits with the idea that culture mediates not only values and meaning but also identity.

Language is not only purposed for the transfer of information. Another aspect of language that makes it more tool-like is that we actually use language to *accomplish* something.

For example, the words "I now pronounce you man and wife" perform the function of marrying a couple. And the words "I nominate Rebecca as team captain" have actually *done* something. When one person says to another, "I hate you," we say, "Those were hurtful words," because the words didn't just transfer the state of hatred—they actually functioned to wound the hearer. Linguists use the term "speech acts" to describe this aspect of language[5] and they have identified dozens of things we *do* with language: we confess, forgive, frighten, inspire, and so on.

So it turns out that what I thought was special about programming—creating and doing things with language—is not so unique after all. From the opening pages of Genesis, we find God speaking the entire universe into existence and Adam making up words as his first creative acts. Language is our first example of how humans create within the creation of God, imbuing each creation with value and meaning. God designed the world in such a way to be cultivated and shaped by humanity, and when we create we are operating as God's image-bearers.

Sadly, we don't get to stay in the perfection of the Garden of Eden for long. We have to move on to Genesis 3 and the fall, a world in which our creativity is tainted by sin and sinfulness. But first, we need to spend some time distinguishing technology from other elements of culture. To do that, I'll take you to a dinner party in north Dallas.

4

DEFINITION

A few years ago at a housewarming party for a friend, I met the CEO of an up-and-coming technology company who also happens to be a passionate Christian man. Since our interests overlapped, we started a lively discussion about technology and culture.

As we were talking about the direction technology will take us in the coming years, he stopped abruptly and said, "Wait a minute. That would mean we'd have to consider just about *everything* to be technology—cars, boats, phones, air-conditioning, and on and on." In that moment, we both realized that we'd been using the word *technology* with slightly different meanings. For him, the term *technology* meant electronic gadgets like mobile phones, iPods, laptops, GPS, and HDTVs, but it didn't include mechanically oriented things like cars, espresso machines, and microwaves. Yet he also said things like, "My company offers more advanced technological solutions than any of our competitors." In that case, he wasn't using "technology" to refer to physical gadgets but more broadly to the kind of "high-tech knowledge" that businesses use to solve problems.

So what is "technology" exactly? Does it refer only to electronics or does it include mechanical devices as well? Can it also mean a special kind of working knowledge? Even if we could answer this, today's technology seems far removed from the biblical command to cultivate the garden and from the kinds of tools used by biblical characters like Moses and Isaiah. Is there any relationship between the technology of the Scriptures and technology today?

The following pages will equip you for thrilling dinner conversations by narrowing down where technology fits into the commands to cultivate the earth and serve as God's image-bearers. First, by briefly tracing the historical usage of the word *technology,* we'll look at how we arrived at such confusion over its meaning. Next we'll attempt to compare ancient tools to today's enormously complex technology by dissecting it into four components. And finally, we propose a simple definition of technology that we can use in the rest of the book.

Origins of "Technology"

The English term *technology* is composed of two Greek words: *téchnē,* which means "craft, skill, or art," and *logía,* which refers to the systematic study of a subject. But unlike the way we have been discussing technology, the Greek term *téchnē* referred to a person's skill in making things, not the tools they used to do so.

When we say someone is "into technology," we usually mean they own a lot of new devices and enjoy using them, but when the Greeks called someone a *tektōn* (in chapter 9, we'll find that this was the term used to describe the occupation of Jesus' father Joseph), it meant that the person had spent a great deal of time learning and honing a particular craft. That craft could be working with wood, stone, metal, or some other physical material. Since there were no factories to mass-produce things, every painting, every knife, every sculpture, and every horseshoe was a unique work that reflected the maker's *téchnē.*

Téchnē could even refer to writing poetry or drafting plans. In fact, the only ancient writer to combine the words *téchnē* and *logía* into our term *technologia* was the philosopher Aristotle who used the word to describe the systematic study of grammar, speech, and writing. The Greeks and the ancient world in general did not distinguish between art and technology as we do today but grouped them together with a wider range of skills and knowledge.

It wasn't until much later during the 1600s when the term *technology* found its way into the English language. At that time, people used it in much the same way that the Greeks did, referring to any skill or craft that a person might learn. But the 1600s was also a turning point in history with its explosion in scientific knowledge, and inventors started experimenting with the first large-scale machinery. Up to this point, almost every tool in existence was small enough for a single individual to use, but these newer, larger machines needed wind, water, or animals to power them. The new machines also gave humanity unprecedented new powers to manipulate and process the materials of the earth, and this led scientists like Galileo and philosophers like Descartes to begin speaking in terms of "crafting" the world and "shaping" it according to the needs of humanity.

For the first time, humans saw their abilities extend beyond cultivating their little plots of land to actually dominating the natural world. Over time, as these machines grew larger and more powerful, people started distinguishing between "fine arts" like painting and sculpting and the "mechanical arts" (i.e., machine making). Eventually, they stopped using the word *technology* to refer to crafting skills, and began using it exclusively in reference to mechanical arts.

Previously the skill of mechanical arts had been passed down from experienced master blacksmiths to younger men through a process of apprenticeship. But during the Industrial Revolution of the 1700s and 1800s, large factories began to pop up all over Europe. These factories could produce thousands of identical goods much faster than individual blacksmiths could produce unique works. As blacksmiths shuttered their doors, apprenticeship as a means of teaching was also pushed aside in favor of a more formal setting for distributing skills. Factories needed workers who had the same knowledge and skill sets so that they could be easily interchanged; therefore education needed to be standardized.

This led to people using the word *technology* to refer to studying the mechanical arts in a formal educational setting. Up to this point, technology meant *practicing* the mechanical arts (i.e., making things), but in this period it came to mean the *study of* the mechanical arts. Harvard professor Jacob Bigelow is credited with being the first to use technology this way in his textbook *Elements of Technology* published in 1829. A few decades later in 1861, the Massachusetts Institute of Technology was founded with this educational meaning of technology embedded in its name.

At the end of the 1800s, technology still meant either practicing or studying mechanical arts, but no one was using it to refer to tools as we do today. This all changed in the early 1900s when people started using the word *technology* both for the *tools* used in mechanical arts (such as wrenches and welders) as well as the *things* made by mechanical arts (chairs, cars, boats, and so on). If you're keeping track, this means that technology now has at least four different meanings: (1) the *skill* of making things, (2) the *study* of the skill of making things, (3) the *tools* used to make things, and (4) the *things* made with these tools.

Part of this confusion arose because many European languages had multiple, distinct terms for these aspects of the single English word *technology*. For example, German and French use the word *technologie* to refer to the study of making industrial products, but they have different words (*arts et métiers* in French and *Technik* in German) to refer to actually making those industrial products.

Exponential Growth

Another reason *technology* came to refer to so many things is that the complexity of these tools was increasing at an incredible rate. Historians say that from the dawn of human history until around 1650, the rate of technological change was relatively flat. New inventions—aqueducts, gunpowder, or the printing press—would come along every few hundred years, but 1650 kicked off three distinct ages of tremendous increase in technological innovation: the period from 1650 to 1850, from 1850 to 1950, and from 1950 to 2000.

Long before 1650, when someone invented a new tool, it was used only in the same general region where it was invented, as there was not transportation or communication in place to quickly share it with the rest of the world. But in the period of time leading up to 1650, the world's transportation and communication infrastructure progressed in leaps and bounds. Printed books allowed people to share scientific knowledge and technological skill much faster than before, and that knowledge could be quickly transported around the world using newer, more reliable ships. Each new invention and discovery expanded on the previous ones, leading to a more rapid pace of development. To top it off, the population of the world doubled from 1650 to 1850.

But 1850 didn't mark a slowdown in technology. Rather, the world saw another major increase in technological development. In the century from 1850 to 1950, the population of the earth doubled again, and the foundational technology for almost every tool we use today was invented. While the period from 1650 to 1850 was primarily focused on building larger and more powerful machines far stronger than any human, 1850 to 1950 was focused on replicating the human senses. Whereas the machine age produced mechanical arms and legs, the next hundred years produced electronic eyes, ears, and brains.

The electronic eye came in the form of the photograph (which was initially purely mechanical). Though attempts at photography had gone on for centuries, the technology was finally perfected in this era. And those first cameras paved the way for every iteration of visual technology we have today, from the earliest televisions to today's 3D movies. Electronic ears and mouths came in the form of Edison's phonograph, the first device to capture and play back sounds. Before that time, music could only be experienced in a live setting, and verbal communication could only take place face-to-face. The first electronic brains also found their origin in this time period with the invention of the telegraph. For the first time, information could be transported instantaneously from any place in the world to another. Knowledge was no longer confined to the speed of a horse or a ship but could be shared in an instant.

Then, during the next fifty years from 1950 to 2000, the world's population again doubled, and the microchip accelerated all the prior inventions to warp speed. Every technology we use today—radios, TVs, cell phones, computers, the Internet, and so on—is all built on the foundational tools created roughly between 1850 and 1950. These technologies are powered by the mechanical processes pioneered from 1650 to 1850.

This means that for the past few centuries both the human population and the complexity and power of technology have been growing exponentially. Our network of technology and resources is so vast today that it's almost unrecognizably different from anything prior to the 1650s. It's even harder to see how today's technology relates to what God said to Adam in the garden. But if we break our technology down into more manageable parts, we'll see that it is still very much related to God's charge to cultivate and keep the earth.

Four Layers of Technology

To help comprehend the enormous complexity of technology today, philosopher Stephen J. Kline has broken it down into four discernible layers, each of which build on one another.[1] We will use his layering as a guide for comparing ancient and modern technology, and then use it to create a definition of technology that encompasses both.

Technology as Hardware. Kline writes that at the most basic level "technology" is the physical pieces of hardware that we use including clocks, shovels, belts, thermometers, guns, and cans of root beer. For Kline, any physical object that does not occur naturally in our world counts as technological hardware. Kline does not take the time to define "natural" and "unnatural," but his words nicely fit the distinction that we found back in Genesis between what God has made and what we make out of God's creation.

If you take a moment to look around you, you'll probably find a combination of both "natural" things like people, pets, and plants, as well as "unnatural" things like chairs, beds, desks, lights, water fountains, and so on. According to Kline's definition, all of these human-made goods would be considered technology, making them similar to Grenz's category of "things" or Andy Crouch's "cultural goods." This is a good starting point, but notice that it lumps tools together with art and everything else people make. This means that we'll need to define technology in such a way that we can distinguish it from other things people make.

Technology as Manufacturing. Taking a step back from the devices in our pockets and on our desks, Kline's second layer makes a distinction between those pieces of hardware, and the tools and systems used to make the hardware, such as factories and assembly lines. "Technology as manufacturing" includes the vat holding the molten steel for our cars, the robots that put together computers, and even the complex sociotechnical systems that need to be in place for the factories to operate. This includes everything from the people running the machines to the electrical grid powering the plant to the legislation that regulates the industry.

This layer of technology is significant because it was largely nonexistent before the Industrial Revolution. Most of the tools before that era could be used on their own without support from a large, complex network. Once a knife or a shovel was made, it was useful by itself. But most of the tools we use today like computers and cell phones are useless without batteries, power outlets, cell phone towers, the Internet, and so on. Similarly, building a modern automobile takes entire systems of metal purification, computer programming, and oil and gas production.

Another difference between today's technology and the technology of the past is that the tools used before the 1800s involved mostly the basic materials that Adam could have found lying around the Garden of Eden. This meant that one person could design, build, and use a tool. In contrast, modern technology uses a variety of exotic materials that the average person knows little about. It now takes an army of designers, manufacturers,

transporters, and retailers to create and distribute a piece of modern technology. As our tools grow more and more complex, the network of people
and machines needed to make them grows as well, sometimes spanning
multiple continents.

Our understanding of technology, then, needs to encompass both the
kinds of hardware used in earlier eras as well as the more complex, interconnected systems that make our life possible today. It also forces us to
acknowledge that the tools we use today don't exist in isolation but are
deeply integrated with the lives of those around us.

Technology as Methodology. Kline's third layer of "technology" is the knowledge and know-how necessary for making technological products. This
usage of technology refers neither to the physical products, nor the machines
used to make the products, but the routines, methods, and skills used in the
process of making modern hardware and doing modern business.

Most companies and churches have quite a bit of hardware, but they also
need an "IT guy" who actually has the specialized knowledge of how it all
works. At a higher level, consulting firms make billions of dollars refining
and streamlining the methods (or "business processes") that companies use
to make their hardware. When the company IBM was first created, it actually made "international business machines," but later found that building machines was no longer profitable. In response, IBM transformed itself
into a "technology firm," advertising specialized knowledge that can make
businesses run more efficiently. (My CEO friend at the dinner party was
referring to this layer of technology when he talked about what his business
could offer others.)

This layer of technology is often the most overlooked, but like all "rituals" we create, it too has the capacity to influence the way we see the world.
Theologian Jacques Ellul, whom we will address more in the next chapter,
worried that technology as methodology often shapes our emotional, spiritual, and relational worlds in ways that aren't always compatible with our
Christian faith.

He wrote that in the modern world we have become so accustomed to technological thinking (what he called *La Technique*) that we apply what technology values to almost every problem without even realizing it. For example, Neil Postman wrote that it was not until 1792 that the first numerical grade was given in a school setting.[2] That year, William Farish, a tutor at the University of Cambridge, tried to come up with a uniform way of evaluating students that was as consistent as what a machine would produce. Instead of tracking the progress of each student individually and holistically, Farish applied technological ideas to education, and as a result created the numerical ranking of student progress that we still use today. It now seems impossible to even conceive of modern education without grades. According to Ellul and Postman the more we use technology, the more it mediates to us the value of addressing problems with technological solutions. When we encounter something that doesn't work, we immediately search for a technological method or tool that can solve it, further reinforcing technology's importance in our lives.

We even apply this kind of machinelike thinking to problems that arise in the church. For example, when we apply *La Technique* to the Great Commission to "make disciples," the result is often the creation of a "discipleship program." Churches urge their members to go through the program in hope that they will all come through the process as uniformly mature Christians. Of course, it's wonderful when everyone in our church gets the chance to be theologically and biblically educated, but we can easily err into treating the spiritual growth of a human soul as if it were a simple, mechanical process. Then when we purchase "proven tools for spiritual growth" that don't seem to "work," we assume that we need to find and purchase a different tool, never considering that such a thing might not exist.

I don't mean to be critical of biblical education as a whole (after all, I create online education software for a living!). I merely mean to point out that technology as methodology operates powerfully beneath the surface, often encouraging us to apply the values and priorities of machines to the human soul. When we think about defining technology, we need to remember that it's not just the physical goods that are important but also the way they teach us to think.

Technology as Social Usage. Kline's final layer of technology is at the opposite end of the spectrum from *La Technique*. If technology as methodology is the knowledge of how to create hardware, technology as social usage is the customs and rules around how we use the hardware. For example, our society has created a host of conventions around how we should and shouldn't use cars. We have turn signals, speed limits, yielding rules, and dozens of other conventions designed to keep us safe. Before we are granted a license to drive, we have to demonstrate not only that we can operate a car but that we can do so within these socially defined rules.

Most of the tools invented before the machine age did not require complex rules, because those tools generally could not do much harm other than to the person using them. But as technology grows more complex, it gains the ability to affect more people, and that requires increasingly complex social conventions to use technology in harmonious ways.

Here at the social level we will begin to observe some interesting things about the way technology and culture interact. Sometimes a new technology will create an entirely new way of experiencing an older cultural practice. For example, we mentioned that before Edison invented a way to record and play back sound, music was only experienced with live performers. The advent of recorded music eliminated the need for performers to be present and created new social conventions like gathering around the radio to listen to recorded music. Then in 1979, Sony released the first Walkman. Its batteries made music portable, and its headphones meant that for the first time music was primarily experienced by the individual rather than the group. With the advent of the "mix tape," burnable discs, and digital music, the powerful emotional experience of music could now be tailored specifically to the listener.

The result was a role reversal of artist and listener. Instead of the artist controlling the flow of the music, now listeners used playlists to control the order of the artists. People now walk down the street experiencing a world that no one else can see or hear. This creates a culture known only to the individual listener, separated from all other communities.

These examples show us that changes in technology result in changes in culture. These changes are not entirely predictable, however, because the social usage pattern of a technology is often different from the intent of its designers. For example, Twitter was originally designed largely as an interface for sending text messages to a large group of friends. One person would send a message to Twitter, and then Twitter would then disseminate it as a text message to mobile phones subscribed to that specific person. In essence, Twitter was initially designed as a one-way broadcast mechanism.

However, Twitter users began using the service in ways its designers did not entirely foresee. They began using it less and less through text messages and more and more online through the main Twitter website and third party programs. And instead of always broadcasting one-way messages, they began using it for two-way conversations. To make these conversations work, users created their own conventions for how to reply to one another and share messages across groups of friends. Eventually Twitter adopted the @reply standard, as well as a version of the "retweet," but they did so long after these other uses had become social conventions.

The examples of the Walkman and Twitter show us that just as tools both shape the world and their users, technology can also shape entire cultures, and in turn be shaped by those cultures. Individuals within cultures create tools, then others within the culture begin using the tool, creating social conventions around its usage. Those conventions then become incorporated into the culture itself, and over time, the tools and conventions around the tools begin to shape the thinking of the individuals who use them.

Technology Defined

Kline's four layers of technology are helpful in dissecting the complexity of modern technology, showing us how intertwined technology is with almost everything we do, but also how its parts are not entirely different from ancient technology. We are therefore able to create a simple, encompassing definition of technology: "the human activity of using tools to transform God's creation for practical purposes."[3] At just thirteen words, it may not seem like much, so let's unpack it a bit.

First, because technology is more than just the tools we use, we define technology as an "activity" that we do and that we are constantly doing. But we don't do this activity as individuals in isolation. Rather, technology takes place within the context of "human" communities, and when we use technology we must recognize that it affects those around us. Of course, technology involves "using tools," and by "tool" we mean both physical *things* like wrenches, airplanes, and microchips and the *methods* we use to manage them. What makes a tool distinct from other cultural goods is that it is used to "transform God's creation." Many cultural goods like art exist for their own sake, but tools have a job: transforming the natural world. We might say that we *hold* tools, but we *behold* art.

When we use tools for transformation, we do so for some "practical end." This is meant to acknowledge that what we are transforming is God's, but also that humans do so for their own purposes. Sometimes those "ends" are in line with what God would want—balancing the commands to cultivate and to keep—but sometimes people transform the world for their own selfish gain.

To see how the definition works, let's now apply it to a simple tool, like our trusty shovel from chapter 2. The "activity" that we do with a shovel is moving dirt—literally an act of transforming God's creation. But typically people don't dig just for the sake of digging. They dig for some bigger purpose, or a "practical end," such as building a house or burying treasure.

This brings us some additional distinctions that are sometimes helpful when talking about technology. The first is separating *tools* from the *products* of those tools. We can think of a *tool* as what we use to create something and a *product* as the thing we create or consume. For example, a camera is a *tool* because we use it to make something else, but a movie is a *product* because it is something we consume. A paintbrush is a *tool* for creating, but a painting is a *product* that we consume. A skillet is a *tool* to create an omelet, and the omelet itself is a *product*.

It's also helpful to distinguish between tools used to *create* products, tools used to *consume* products, and tools that both create and consume products. For example, a video camera is useful for creating a movie, while a television can only consume the movie. A computer, however, is good at both creating movies and consuming movies, and a fork can be used both to create and consume food.

So where do modern tools like mobile phones and social networks fit into these categories? They certainly have a "practical end," but at first glance they don't really seem to transform God's creation—at least in a physical sense. However, these tools still have a powerful transformative effect on the world as we know it, something I observed firsthand during a recent trip to Oregon.

As a high school student, I was fortunate enough to have a dedicated youth group leader named Scott who took a few friends and me on hiking trips through the mountains of eastern Oregon every summer. Scott taught us how to purify water and cook our own food, but for us teenagers the best part was that we had no way of contacting our family for over a week.

A few years ago, Scott organized a reunion for our group, taking us to the same places we had been ten years before. As I hiked in, I was amazed that the paths, lakes, trees, and mountains hadn't changed much since we had last visited. But it was after dinner that the transformation happened . . . when each of us reached into our packs and got out our phones. We ran around the campsite searching for a good signal, and once we found the "sweet spot," we called our wives and children to tell them about the hike. Those calls didn't transform God's creation in a literal sense like a shovel does, but the mobile phones still performed a very distinct transformative function.

On the surface, all a phone does is transport speech from here to there. But if we think differently about what's happening, the phone is transforming the physical world by connecting two people who are physically distant. In addition, the presence of a cell phone in my pocket means that my conceptions of space, time, and limits are radically different than a world without cell phones. The mountains of eastern Oregon look the same as they did before cell phones, but the way I now experience them and the time with my friends has been transformed by the presence of mobile phone technology.

While a phone only has the power to modify the limits of physical space, other communication technologies go a step further, transforming even time itself. To use a phone for communication, two people have to operate them at the same time, but a tool like the book you are holding allows me to transfer thoughts and ideas without the need for both of us to do something at the same time. A phone allows us to have conversations across physical distances, but books allow us to have a conversation across time. In this sense, the technology of writing—whether in a book or on a website—transforms God's creation by shaping the way we experience both time and space.

Social networks like Facebook likewise have transformative effects on the way we experience the world by taking friendship and personal identity and reforming them into a unified, consistent experience. When we use Facebook, we take who we are and transform our identity into something that fits on a webpage. A profile on Facebook (as of early 2011) prioritizes our job title, educational background, spouse, and hometown, subtly implying that those are the most important parts of who we are. We will examine this idea more closely in chapter 11, but the result is that *we* become the *product* of the *tool* of Facebook. We are not yet attempting to be critical of such tools, only pointing out that tools function as a cultural good, mediating to us certain values, meaning, and identity.

So we have defined technology as "the human activity of using tools to transform God's creation for practical purposes." This is a special subset of the command to create and cultivate the garden, and it began with Adam's creation of language. But as we all know, Adam didn't stay in the garden for long, and we will now begin observing what happens when sin enters the world of technology.

5

REBELLION

The first and last time I ever stole something was when I was ten years old, and I stole a Teenage Mutant Ninja Turtle action figure from Walmart. My mom dropped me off in the toy section so I could use my allowance to buy whatever I wanted, but I didn't bring enough money for the figure I wanted. So, while no one was looking, I slipped one into my bag, and casually walked away to find my mom.

I tried as hard as I could to act like nothing was out of the ordinary, but the sense of exhilaration I felt as we pulled away from Walmart was amazing. However, the closer we got to my house, the more that feeling of exhilaration began transforming into guilt, worry, and regret. That evening I felt so sick I couldn't even eat dinner. I went back to my room to play with the toy I had so desperately wanted a few hours ago, only to find myself wishing that I could undo what I had done.

I imagine that Adam and Eve probably had a similar feeling in the moments after they finished eating the forbidden fruit. Those first few bites were probably pretty enjoyable, but as they got near the end, they would have realized something terrible had happened that could never be undone.

Now put yourself in Adam and Eve's position for a moment. You've just committed the world's first sin, introducing suffering and death to all humanity. What would your first move be?

If we turn our phones on and scroll to Genesis 3, we'll find that Adam and Eve's very first act after sinning simultaneously reflected their programming as God's image-bearers, and their newfound sinfulness. Genesis 3:7 says that as soon as they realized what they had done, their first response was to "make" something—their first set of clothing.

In the first few chapters of Genesis, there are several Hebrew words that describe God's creative acts. Sometimes he "creates,"[1] sometimes he "forms,"[2] and other times he "makes."[3] The most common is that last term *make*, the same word used to describe what Adam and Eve did with the fig leaves. Even in their new sinful state, they didn't lose their status as God's image-bearers, and it is almost as if they couldn't help but start creating.

Together, they transformed a bit of God's creation—fig leaves—into something with a practical purpose. In other words, they started doing technology according to the way we've defined it. Today we don't think of clothing as "technology," but that's because we use it primarily to communicate fashion and status. For Adam and Eve, however, the fig leaves served a purely practical purpose—to protect them from their environment.

But like all human creations, their clothing was not limited to mere *function*. It also had meaning for them, and it represented the new values of their fallen state. Genesis tells us that in the moments after they ate the fruit, Adam and Eve suddenly became aware of their nakedness. Commentators suggest that on the surface this means just what it says—Adam and Eve recognized that they were literally nude and that their physical environment could harm them. But the awareness of their physical nakedness also represents the knowledge that their sin was laid bare before a holy God.

Adam and Eve's clothing, then, was not only designed to protect them from their environment; it also represents their attempt to hide their sinfulness from God. Moreover, they were trying to invent a means by which they could live without God and were therefore acting in rebellion against him. Instead of living every day in a loving, open relationship with him—depending on his power and grace for their existence and joy—they tried to construct a world that would allow them to exist apart from him. The clothing was their way of transforming their circumstances such that they would no longer rely on God for anything.

The clothing also represents a major shift in their relationship with God and one another. From this point forward, Adam and his offspring would no longer walk with God in the garden. Instead, they would always communicate with God *through* something else. It might be a dream, a voice, a book, a prophet, or a miraculous sign; but God's presence would always be mediated in some way. We were designed to experience the nonmediated (or *im*mediate) presence of God, but no human would experience that again for countless generations.

So in this first human invention, we find that technology can at the same time be both a reflection of the image of God and a subtle rebellion against him and his authority. Today nearly every tool available to us enables us to perpetuate the myth that we can live apart from dependence upon God. Instead of affirming that the Son holds every speck of the universe in place, we amass tools with the belief that they can help us overcome our deepest problems. Yet even though Adam and Eve clearly abused their creative powers, we'll soon find out that God didn't condemn them for their technological activity.

The First Technology Upgrade

As they were trying on their new clothes, Adam and Eve heard God walking toward them in the garden. As if hiding behind fig leaves weren't enough, they then tried to hide behind trees, hoping God would pass them by. Of course this didn't work, and what follows is the sad announcement of God's judgment on creation.

We do not have space to adequately treat the gravity of this section of Scripture, but we should be careful to observe that God's curses directly interfere with the commands God had given in Genesis 1 and 2. Pain in childbearing, for example, affects our call to "be fruitful and multiply," and the curse of the ground means that very thing we were called to cultivate is now flawed and broken. From that point forward all of our creative acts and everything we make—even the most advanced of today's technology—will be built from sin-cursed material.

But Genesis 3 is not all bad news for technology. In fact, in the moments before Adam and Eve are kicked out of the garden, there is a bright spot. Before the angels with flaming swords arrive, God takes a look at Adam and Eve's garments, and instead of condemning the misuse of their creative powers and their attempt to solve their problems without him, God responds by doing something amazingly gracious—he gives out the world's first free technology upgrade. He replaces their rough, uncomfortable, and relatively small fig leaves with brand-new state-of-the-art animal skins.

Genesis 2:21 says very matter-of-factly, "And the LORD God made for Adam and for his wife garments of skins and clothed them." Again, the verb *make* shows up, the same one used when God "made" us in his image, when Adam and Eve "made" clothing, and now when the Creator "made" garments for his children. According to our definition of technology as transforming the natural world into useful things, God himself here is "doing technology." Adam and Eve transformed fig leaves, but God transformed animal skins.[4] And in doing so, God appears to be sanctioning Adam and Eve's inventiveness, even offering them suggestions on how to improve upon it.

It is also significant that God's clothing upgrade comes just after he curses the environment, but before he removes them from the garden and sends them off into the harsh, new wilderness. God's grace is evident in this because immediately after sin begins to take its toll on creation, God provides a means of lessening the effects of that curse.

In some sense, all of our technology can be understood as an attempt to overcome the effects of the fall. We create shovels and tractors to help us work the unruly land, and we invent soft bedding and epidurals to help ease the pain of childbearing. We build air conditioners and heaters to overcome the weather and drive-through windows to overcome our hunger. We invent lightbulbs to overcome the darkness and search engines to overcome our lack of wisdom. Each of these inventions brings us incredible benefits, and collectively they work to reduce the suffering that we experience from the curses of the fall. And yet, like Adam and Eve's clothing, our technology never truly solves the deeper problem of sin that came with the fall.

This is why many theologians believe that in creating the animal skin clothing, God was foreshadowing the means by which he would overcome the spiritual consequences of the fall. Adam and Eve tried to fix their sin problem with leaves, but God was giving them a visual picture of what the author of Hebrew would later write, "without shedding of blood there is no forgiveness of sins" (Heb. 9:22). God was saying that no amount of technological activity—even when God himself is doing it—will ever fully overcome the curses of the fall.

So God accomplished three things with the clothing he made. First, he affirmed that even after the fall humanity is called to use its creativity to continue cultivating his creation. Even those of us who believe in "total depravity"—that every part of our humanity is infected with sin—believe that the most sinful person among us is made in the image of God and that every creative act is a reflection of the one who imparted creativity to us. When Steve Jobs (Apple CEO) creates a beautiful, functional device, even he is reflecting the image of God (even though he does not profess Christianity). Second, God made it known that from time to time he will participate with humanity in doing technology. Sometimes he will help us ease the effects of the fall, and other times he will use technology more disruptively as a means of carrying out his plan of redemption. Finally, God was saying that while technology can temporarily ease some of our pain, we must not be so foolish as to make it our ultimate source of hope. Technology does not have the power to save. God alone will do that, and it will be quite costly for him.

Today our technological creations still honor God, and they are still a reflection of his creativity. But we must be careful not to believe the lie that the right tools will enable us to live independent from our Creator, the sustainer of life. Medicine may help us live longer, but we all still die in the end. And microphones might help us reach more people, but only a movement of God's Spirit can save them.

The deception of technological salvation was born out of those fig leaves, and as we pick up the biblical story outside the garden, we will find this deception growing ever stronger.

The Anti-Gardener

I am the oldest of three brothers, which means that while growing up I was in the enviable position of being able to beat up on my brothers whenever I pleased. However, this all changed when I entered high school and my middle brother started gaining on me. Thankfully, I left for college before he outgrew me, and today, I'm happy to report we have a great relationship.

Stepping into Genesis 4, we see that brotherly conflict is nothing new. As we all know, the story of Cain and Abel didn't turn out as well as it did for me and my brothers. When Cain and Abel brought their offerings before God, God approved of Abel's and rejected Cain's. This incensed Cain, and even after God warned him about the power of sin and temptation, Cain retaliated by killing his brother.

Interestingly, Genesis doesn't tell us why God rejected Cain's offering. The only obvious difference comes in the content of their offerings—Cain brought crops, and Abel brought an animal. But the laws of Israel allow both animal and plant offerings, so there isn't anything obviously wrong with what Cain brought. In fact, Genesis suggests his offering might have been superior to Abel's. Looking at their job descriptions, Abel is called "keeper of sheep," but Cain gets the title "worker of the ground" (Gen. 4:2), a direct reference to the words "man to work the ground" in Genesis 2:5. Cain, then, is doing word-for-word what God designed humanity to do on earth, and yet his sacrifice was rejected.

Thankfully, the author of Hebrews comes through again for us when he writes that the issue was not between crops and blood but between faith and faithlessness. He writes, "By faith Abel offered to God a more acceptable sacrifice than Cain, through which he was commended as righteous, God commending him by accepting his gifts" (Heb. 11:4). The apostle John also weighs in, using Cain as an example of doing evil when he writes, "We should not be like Cain, who was of the evil one and murdered his brother. And why did he murder him? Because his own deeds were evil and his brother's righteous" (1 John 3:12).

This situation teaches another lesson about creating and doing technology. Just as Adam and Eve showed that they could do technology for good even in their sinful state, Cain illustrates that we can do good technology in a faithless, sinful way. Cain was following the letter of the law when it came to the culture mandate, and externally there was nothing wrong with what he made from the world. Yet John and Hebrews tell us God rejected Cain's work for the sole reason that it wasn't offered in faith.

Today we, too, can create helpful, productive, and even redemptive technology, but if we don't offer and use it in faith, it is worthless. God will reject our work just as he rejected Cain's. But the story of Cain doesn't end with the killing of his brother. What he does next is perhaps even more instructive in regard to technology.

The Anti-Garden

The episode that follows between Cain and God mirrors what happened between God and Cain's parents. First, God questions Cain, then Cain makes excuses. God responds with curses, and then Cain is forced to move even farther away from the garden.

Back in Genesis 3, God told Adam, "*The ground is cursed* because of you"; but here God intensifies the curse, telling Cain, "*You are cursed* from the ground. . . . When you work the ground, it shall no longer yield to you its strength" (Gen. 4:11–12). The ground is personified here, as God states that it will continually curse Cain. I can almost imagine Cain attempting to put a seed in the ground, and the ground spitting it back at him.

In Genesis 2, 3, and 4 the language of "cultivate the ground" is repeated over and over again, but with each successive sin the ability to do it is tainted and damaged, putting further distance between humanity and God's design. But God also puts literal distance between Cain and the ability to enjoy the bounty of creation. He tells Cain, "You shall be a fugitive and a wanderer on the earth" (Gen. 4:12). Cain had been designed to be at home in the garden, but God was now telling Cain that he would never have a home. Cain had been designed to have dominion over creation, but now the earth would dominate him. He was created to multiply and fill the earth, but instead he chose to reduce the human population. The consequences of his actions were that he had no brother, no friends, and no home.

So how does Cain respond to all of this? First, he negotiates with God to protect his life, and God, in his grace, offers to protect him. But then comes a curious little verse: "Then Cain went away from the presence of the LORD and settled in the land of Nod, east of Eden" (Gen. 4:16). Remember, God had placed angels with flaming swords on the east side of the Garden of Eden (Gen. 3:24) keeping Adam and Eve out. Now God forced Cain to go even farther east and farther away from the garden. In Hebrew the word "Nod" sounds like the word for "wanderer," and many commentators think that the "land of Nod" is a metaphor meant to portray Cain entering a "state of wandering." The picture is that he was literally and figuratively moving farther and farther away from God, the garden, and who he was designed to be. He, like all of us in a sinful world, would never be able to return to his true home; and the more he sinned, the more physically and spiritually alienated he became.

But Cain was still a human being, commanded to multiply and create. And in the next verse, we find that Cain does just that. Genesis 4:17 says that Cain and his wife had a child. But even more importantly, Cain does something that had never been done before—he "built a city." At some point, Cain apparently decided to stop wandering so he could build a permanent place to live. As we've said before, our acts of "making" represent our values and identity, and Cain's city was no exception. It reflected what he wanted from the world, and how he felt that life should be.

In his book *The Meaning of the City*, theologian Jacques Ellul explores how the concept of the city is treated throughout the Bible. Ellul wrote that in building the first city, Cain was attempting to set up an alternative to the Garden of Eden. Instead of a place where humans lived in relationship with God, deeply connected to him and his creation, Cain built a place where people could live without God and disconnect from his creation. In building his city, Cain collected as many tools and resources as he could find and attempted to create a place of safety and comfort, a place where he could be protected from the natural world and insulated from his need for God. Ellul writes:

> For when man is faced with a curse he answers, "I'll take care of my problems." And he puts everything to work to become powerful, to keep the curse from having its effects. He creates the arts and the sciences, he raises an army, he constructs chariots, he builds cities. The spirit of might is a response to the divine curse.[5]

In building his city, Cain was obviously doing technology. He was using tools to transform God's creation for practical ends, and like his parents he both fulfilled his role as an image-bearer while at the same time living in rebellion against God. Although we would prefer to think of cities as merely a practical means of sharing human resources, they often come to represent much more to us.[6] Ellul points out that the Bible consistently portrays cities as places of evil, disconnected from God and creation. When Jesus addressed people, he offered blessings to some and curses to others, but when he mentioned cities, it was always in the context of judgment.

This is in part because the city is humankind's first idol, the first attempt to use our creative powers to dislodge God from his place of preeminence and his rightful status as the sustainer of life. We use our idols fundamentally as a way of meeting our needs apart from God, and this is our greatest temptation with technology—to use it as a substitute for God.

The fifth-century theologian Augustine wrote that all sin is an "incurvature of the soul" or a turning inward toward the self.[7] Technology, for all its good, often amplifies and augments this inward turn. In *The City of God*, Augustine goes on to say of the city that, "By craving to be more, man becomes less; and by aspiring to be self-[sufficient], he fell away from Him who is [truly sufficient for him]."[8]

We also use our idols, especially our technological ones, as a means of distraction. When we find something that offers us temporary relief from the curse of sin, instead of allowing its shortcomings to make us long for our Savior, we allow the technology to distract us from our obvious need of a savior. Blaise Pascal, the seventeenth-century philosopher and mathematician, captured our tendency toward distraction when he wrote, "When I have occasionally set myself to consider the different distractions of men . . . I have discovered that all the unhappiness of men arises from one single fact, that they cannot stay quietly in their own chamber."[9] Cain distracted himself with the tools of his day, and we distract ourselves with our ever-present televisions, constantly buzzing phones, and endless Internet surfing. From Cain's city to our modern electronics, we are constantly seeking something that will distract us from coming to terms with the fact that we are all inhabitants of the land of Nod. We'll return to the theme of this city later, but for now let's see what technological applications emerge from the study of it.

The First Technological Revolution

Long before the revolutions of gunpowder, the printing press, and the Internet, Genesis 4 tells us the story of the first technological revolution. Here in the city that Cain built to escape God, the Bible tells us that there was a technological and cultural explosion. Cain continued having children, and we find that his grandchildren went on to develop the three major strands of human culture:

> Adah bore Jabal; he was the father of those who dwell in tents and *have livestock*. His brother's name was Jubal; he was the father of all *those who play the lyre* and pipe. Zillah

also bore Tubal-cain; he was the *forger of all instruments* of
bronze and iron. (Gen. 4:20–22, emphasis added)

Cain's offspring—those born in the anti-garden at the center of humankind's rejection of God—developed (1) animal husbandry, (2) art and
music, and (3) metal tools.[10] Incredibly, these three areas—agriculture, art,
and technology—broadly summarize human culture. Even today, these
three categories apply to how our society operates. We still have the mass
production of food through the farming industry. We still make music,
books, and other forms of art. And of course, we still make and use tools.

The section on Cain ends fittingly with the account of Lamech, another
boastful murderer. But Genesis 4 doesn't end with the evil line of Cain
conquering all. Instead, it ends on a more redemptive note with the birth of
Cain's brother Seth:

And Adam knew his wife again, and she bore a son and
called his name Seth. . . . To Seth also a son was born, and
he called his name Enosh. At that time people began to
call upon the name of the Lord. (Gen. 4:25–26)

In direct contrast to Cain's descendants, all of whom rejected God and
did everything they could to live apart from him, the line of Seth is portrayed as the first to formally worship God. Interestingly, the Bible doesn't
tell us if Seth's descendants created anything or contributed to culture. All
we know about them is that they called upon the name of God.

It's almost as if Genesis is trying to contrast technological and cultural
development with righteousness. Cain and the tool-using, music-playing
pagans are over there, while the simple, backwoods believers are over here.
Does this mean that God is telling us to retreat from creating? Does the
comparison of Cain and Seth suggest that we should stop using technology
and focus more on our worship?

As we'll see in the coming chapters of Genesis, the answer to this question
is definitely no. God will demonstrate that he still wants us to be creators of

cultural goods and doers of technology. And yet, the Cain, Abel, and Seth stories hammer home the point that any act of making divorced from faith is worthless. God cares much more about our faith and the genuineness of our worship than how high tech we are. Sadly, I've often heard people criticize a church, saying, "That church is so behind technologically. It's almost sad!" But I think this passage suggests that God is more interested in our theology of worship than in our technology of worship.

That said, technology and culture do matter in the story of God. And as we move deeper into the Scriptures, and watch God begin his redemptive program, we'll find that technology will often have a small but important role to play. For now, we can summarize what we've found by saying that even in the post-fall world, God not only approves of but even helps with our technological development. At the same time, technology is also one of the chief means by which humans attempt to create a world without God. As our technology grows more and more powerful, the illusion of control becomes increasingly convincing. Today, our powers have grown to the point that in Western industrialized countries, we can go through our entire lives without the slightest physical need for God or other people.

But does all of this mean that technology itself is inherently evil? Does technology *cause* us to do sinful things, or is technology itself simply neutral? In the next chapter, we'll try to answer these questions. We will start with a trip to Austin, Texas.

6

APPROACH

Every spring thousands of musicians, artists, and technology companies head down to Austin, Texas, for the annual South by Southwest (SXSW) conference. SXSW began as a music festival that lived up to Austin's motto of "Keep Austin Weird," but later it added an event for film and then another for interactive media called SXSW Interactive. Since the mid 1990s, SXSW Interactive has been one of the go-to events for companies attempting to launch new websites and mobile devices.

A few days after the 2010 SXSW conference ended, a local Christian radio host decided to open up his program for listeners to call in and discuss how Christians should use and think about technology. The first caller was an older gentleman who talked excitedly about how his church was sending text messages to congregants during the week designed to reinforce the application points from the pastor's sermon. The caller said he initially thought the pastor was crazy for texting about his sermons, but after a receiving a few of the daily texts, he found himself trying harder to apply the message through the week. Both he and the host were impressed that his church was so forward-thinking and creative in their use of technology.

The next caller, however, a mother of three teenagers, wasn't so excited about texting. She quickly rattled several horror stories about sexting (i.e., kids sending sexually explicit pictures of themselves back and forth with their cell phones) in the local school system. In one of those stories, a girl sent an explicit photo of herself to a friend who then shared it with so many people in their school that the girl was forced to leave and start homeschooling. The caller then started to share other worries about how technology was affecting her own kids. She said her kids spent most of their evenings locked away in their rooms playing video games and texting their friends. Through the conversation it was obvious that technology was her enemy. She was saying things like, "Technology is making my kids narcissistic."

Throughout the radio program, these kinds of back and forth stories continued. Some felt that technology was making everything better, citing missionaries doing translation work via satellite. The other half told stories of pornography, affairs on Facebook, and how technology was destroying society and undermining traditional family values.

Toward the end of the program, the host tried to calm down the audience a bit, telling them that they needed to remember that technology itself is neither good nor evil. We can't blame technology for our problems, he said, because technology itself is simply neutral. What matters is that we try to use our technology in a way that glorifies God and furthers the gospel. As long as we aren't using technology for selfish purposes, then we can make it into a force for good as opposed to evil.

After what we've seen in the Scriptures about technology, what do you think about what the radio host had to say? Was he right in saying that technology is neither good nor evil but simply neutral? How does this square with God's original command to create culture, part of which is doing technology? And what about the city of Cain, and humanity's attempts to live apart from God using technology?

Neutrality and Gray Areas

The radio host's final words represented a fairly common way that people, particularly Christians, think about technology. And there's good reason for that—it makes a lot of sense within a Christian view of the world. We believe that God is holy, and that he cares about our holiness, so we are rightly concerned with issues of right and wrong. We also believe that inanimate objects like shovels and cell phones are not moral creatures, and they cannot force us do anything. We alone, not machines, are responsible for our choices.

When we come across an activity that can't be clearly classified as morally good or morally bad, we put that activity in a special category called a "gray area." Into this category we put things like watching R-rated movies, getting tattoos, and voting for a certain party. Since we can't make universal statements about whether these choices are clearly black or white, we say that they are "gray," and tell individuals to take them up with God.

Because technology is not black or white, we tend to put it in the "gray area" category as well. The presence or absence of a phone in our pockets is neither morally good nor morally evil, so we tend to categorize the device as being "neutral." Once we've declared the device itself to be neutral, we then ignore the device itself and focus only on whether we are using it for good or bad purposes. We believe that as long as you use the phone to call good people and not to do something like arm a bomb on a plane, then you have nothing to worry about.

But is this really all we can say about technology? More importantly, is this all we *should* say about technology? While the viewpoint of our radio host is certainly well meaning, it short-circuits the kind of deeper discussion about technology that we must have in order to live faithfully in today's world. For those who insist that technology is neutral, Marshall McLuhan has some strong words: "Our conventional response to all media, namely that it is how they are used that counts, is the numb stance of the technological idiot."[1] I'm guessing that none of us want to be idiots, especially not technological idiots, so we need to spend some time developing ways to talk about technology without limiting our discussion to how we should use it.

Philosophy of Technology 101

In his book *The Whale and the Reactor*, Langdon Winner wrote, "At this late date in the development of our industrial/technological civilization the most accurate observation to be made about the philosophy of technology is that there really isn't one."[2] But while Winner may be correct that there is not a single agreed upon philosophy of technology, most people— including those who called into the radio program—approach technology through a particular philosophy whether they realize it or not. In fact the host and callers represented two distinct philosophies of technology that we will examine below. There are dozens of theories and finely nuanced viewpoints in the study of technology, but they can be summarized into two extreme poles with several intermediate viewpoints somewhere in between.

At one end of the spectrum is *instrumentalism,* a view very similar to what the radio host unknowingly espoused. Instrumentalism gets its name from the belief that technology is merely the instrument of the person using it. The tool itself is neutral in that it is interchangeable with any other tool with no effect.

Instrumentalism is often expressed in the popular notion that, "Guns don't kill people. People kill people." This pithy saying is arguing that guns should not receive any blame when one person kills another. The gun is simply the instrument the killer chose to use, but the killer could have exchanged it for any other weapon. Therefore there is no need to worry about the presence or absences of guns, only how people use them.

This argument certainly has a ring of truth to it. People are in fact responsible for their actions, and societies put people in jail, not guns. Yet while clever and popular, this bumper sticker slogan doesn't tell the whole story about how guns and people interact.

There are dozens of studies arguing back and forth about whether societies with guns are more violent than those without guns, and I don't intend to get into that here. What I do want to point out is that guns do have an effect on people even when they are not in use. Whatever our beliefs about guns in society, we must acknowledge that a home with a gun is a different place than one without a gun. When we bring a gun into a home, we also bring with it a set of cultural practices (Kline's "technology as social practice" from chapter 4) such as keeping it locked away, never pointing it at anyone, and only touching the trigger when you are ready to fire. Even if the gun is never taken out of its case, the presence of a gun commands a different way of life than a life without guns.

Guns are not unique in this regard. In fact, every technology brings with it a set of conventions and new choices that alter the way we live. And this leads us to the view of technology at the opposite end of the spectrum from instrumentalism.

This second view, called *technological determinism*, says that technology is an unstoppable power that has become the driving force in society. While instrumentalism claims that technology is completely inert and has no operative power in culture, determinism makes the opposite argument, saying that technology operates independently of human choices. Determinists go so far as to say that technology is the primary basis of and reason for societal and cultural change.

Determinism shows up popularly with this statement: "Technology *makes* us . . ." finished by blaming technology for some cultural ill. This was essentially what the callers who worried about technology were saying. But it's not just people who call into radio programs that think this. Bookshelves are filling up with authors claiming that technology, particularly newer things like the Internet, is responsible for just about every problem we have. The implication is that if we remove the technology, the problem will go away, because technology *is* the problem.

But not all technological determinists see technology as a negative force. In fact, one of the most famous technological determinists, Karl Marx, wrote that technology would be the great force that equalized humanity.

He is famous for saying that the windmill was responsible for eliminating the feudal system, and he believed that future technological advances might eliminate poverty and power altogether. Other determinists interpret technology as the primary means of perpetuating human evolution. Once our ancestors developed enough brain capacity to create tools, they no longer needed claws or long teeth. This allowed them to evolve even larger brains, which enabled them to develop more powerful tools, and so on. Some believe that biological evolution has stopped and that the next stage of humanity will come when we develop tools that will enable us to escape the need for material bodies.

Obviously, determinism won't do for Christians who believe that God, not technology, is the sovereign, driving force in history. But many philosophers of technology disagree with this view as well. MIT professor Leo Marx has written:

> We amplify the hazardous character of the concept by investing it with agency—by using the word technology as the subject of active verbs. Take, for example, a stock historical generalization such as: "the cotton-picking machine transformed the southern agricultural economy and set off the Great Migration of black farm workers to northern cities." Here we tacitly invest a machine with the power to initiate change, as if it were capable of altering the course of events, of history itself.[3]

This leads us to a middle ground position on technology. We don't want to say that technology is inert like the instrumentalists, and we don't want to claim that technology is responsible for everything like the determinists. Instead we want to acknowledge that individuals and cultures interact with technology in a complex way. Both determinism and instrumentalism have elements of truth to them, but we cannot reduce all discussions about technology in either direction. People are culpable for their choices, but technology still plays a role in influencing the decisions they make.

Tendencies and Extensions

One way of charting a middle course between determinism and instrumentalism is to say that people are free to choose how they will use their tools, but that the tools themselves are oriented toward a particular set of uses that will emerge when a large number of people use them. For example, when people have lights, they tend to turn them on at night. When people have cell phones, they tend to answer them when a call comes in. A person is free to use a phone as a paperweight, doorstop, or hammer, but people will tend to use phones to accomplish what they were designed to do—communicate with people.

The longer a tool has been around and the more often we use it, the more ingrained and culturally acceptable its tendencies become. Individuals are still free to discard it or use it in some way other than its original design, but the tool has a specific tendency that will usually prevail among the masses. For example, when mobile phones first came on the market, most people bought them only for emergency or business use. Yet, it seems that mobile phones have the built-in tendency to be used much more often, especially as they continue to gain features far beyond making calls. Instrumentalism is partially true in the sense that individuals are free to use phones however they please, but determinism also has an element of truth in that society at large tends to use the technology in a certain way.

In his later years, Marshall McLuhan offered us what he called a "tetrad" that is helpful in understanding how those tendencies emerge and play out within a culture. McLuhan's tetrad proposes that all media and technology do four things. First, they *extend* or *magnify* something that we do naturally. For example, a mobile phone extends our ability to communicate and enhances our sense of personal identity. Second, they *eliminate* or *amputate* something that we used to do. Mobile phones eliminate the need for landlines, and they also eradicate one's ability to be unreachable and alone. Third, all media *retrieves* something from the past. Mobile phones retrieve the ability to connect on a regular basis with a frequency and familiarity that people were accustomed to when they lived in small villages. Finally, every technology has the possibility of *reversing into* a more negative behavior when it's overused. When we use mobile phones too much, we never deeply connect with anyone, and instead we may maintain surface communication with everyone.

McLuhan's four questions about media can be applied to any tool from cars to Twitter, and going through the exercise can help us surface both the benefits and problems with technology. For example, a calculator *extends* our ability to do math, but it *amputates* the need to memorize multiplication tables. By doing math for us, the calculator *retrieves* time, yet when we use it too much we *reverse into* not being able to do basic math ourselves. McLuhan's intent was not to demonize any of our tools or to say that one was better than another, but only to help us understand how we tend to use these tools, and possibly help us avoid problems. Based in part on McLuhan's work, an entire discipline called "media ecology" was created to help catalog and understand these types of interactions.

Media Ecology

When a species is introduced into a biological ecosystem, the presence of that new species affects all the other plants and animals in the system. For example, if you drop a shark into a fish tank, the shark won't simply be added alongside the other fish. Instead, there will a major clash, changing the makeup and order of the fish tank.

Neil Postman used to say, "Technology is ecological, not additive," by which he meant that introducing a new technology into society also changed the makeup of the technological ecosystem. He and his mentor Marshall McLuhan created an academic discipline called "media ecology" to study these changes.

A good place to see how media functions like an ecosystem is the music industry. In the 70s, music lovers brought their favorite songs home on either vinyl records or eight track tapes. Then in the 80s, we shifted over to the cassette tape, which brought us the ability to copy and record our own music, including making the iconic mix tape. The 90s brought us the CD and better music clarity, and then the new millennium brought us digital downloads. Each new iteration of music technology made it easier to buy, listen to, and record music. McLuhan's technological idiot would say that records, tapes, CDs, and MP3s are themselves simply neutral tools. What matters, the idiot tells us, is the content of the music. We should limit ourselves to considering whether the lyrics and beats are pleasing God, but we should ignore the medium through which we access it.

However, if you read any news or history about iTunes, you'll undoubtedly come across statements like "iTunes is *changing the way* we buy music." Some articles talk about how digital downloads enabled consumers to find lesser-known bands that would never have found an audience just by touring around the country. For example, one of my friends plays in a band called Air Review. In the past, they would only have a fan following in the Dallas area, but digital downloads have extended their reach all over the world to places they will never visit.

In addition to extending the reach of bands, when people use iTunes they also tend to change the way they buy and consume music. Today consumers tend to buy fewer full-length albums and instead purchase more individual songs. The concept of an "album" and the arrangement of its songs matters less today than it did with records and CDs. In addition, marketers cannot count on a rush to big stores to buy millions of copies of new CDs since consumers now have a much wider selection of bands online. In the 1990s, producers were constantly trying to find the next boy band who would sell millions of CDs in the first week, but that model doesn't work in the digital world. In fact, since the advent of digital downloads, music stores like Tower Records and Blockbuster Music have gone bankrupt.

Together, all of these little changes mean that the music industry is a very different place than it was a few decades ago. The musical tastes of consumers have certainly changed over time, but for music executives what matters is that the presence of digital downloads tends to influence consumers toward different consumption patterns that push out old mediums like CDs and reshape the technological ecosystem. More recently, the introduction of e-book readers like the Amazon Kindle and iPad have started to reshape the way people buy and consume books, which has led traditional brick-and-mortar bookstores like Borders to go into bankruptcy.

Certainly, digital music downloads are *morally* neutral, yet it doesn't seem helpful or accurate to call iTunes "neutral." We don't want to err into determinism and argue that iTunes *made* anyone do anything, but neither do we want to err into instrumentalism and say that iTunes doesn't matter. Instead, we need to remind ourselves that it's not just music that is an important element of culture but also our musical devices. When our devices change, our culture changes, and then the things people do in our culture changes as well.

While it's fun to know how technology changes businesses like the music industry, iTunes and digital downloads don't directly affect our spiritual lives. However, there have been changes in media and technology that have influenced the way Christians experience church and community life.

Think back for a moment to what church life would have been like in the 1850s. There were no cars, so it would only be feasible to travel a few miles on Sunday morning. This meant that the number of churches you could choose from would be pretty limited, and most congregations would be fairly small. Today, however, we have cars that allow us to travel to any church we want in just a few minutes. A horse-drawn wagon would allow you to travel a maximum of five miles in an hour, but a car makes your travel radius almost infinite. Many of us also live in densely packed areas, making the number of churches we have access to much higher than at any point in human history. This enables some people to go to one church for the preaching, and then drive to another for their community group, something that would have been impossible a century ago.

The combination of the presence of the automobile and the density of our cities results in a quite different set of choices about how and where we do church today. Yet none of us would claim that the choice of where we go to church is morally or spiritually neutral.

And it's not just *where* we go to church that has been influenced by automobiles—*how* we do church has changed as well. If we fast-forward from the 1850s to the 1940s, automobiles are suddenly everywhere in

America. At the time, churches were still relatively small, but if word spread that a preacher was particularly compelling or the music was great, automobiles made it possible for lots of people to go check out the church. However, this created a problem. Churches were mostly small buildings designed to hold only a few people. And most preachers only had the voice capacity to be heard by a few hundred people at the most. If more than that showed up with their new cars, neither the building nor the preacher's voice could accommodate them.

During this same transition, evangelists like Billy Sunday and Billy Graham began holding rallies in stadiums employing a special new set of technologies—the microphone and the speaker. The stadiums and speakers allowed them to reach the huge audiences who drove to see them. Eventually, beginning in the 1950s, churches began to incorporate these technological developments and the result was the birth of the first megachurches. Churches erected huge, stadium-like buildings and used speakers and video to reach all the people who drove there.

However, when we use technology to solve the problem of how to reach thousands of people in the same place on Sunday morning, a new problem pops up—how do we get all these people to know each other? Can we really call it "community" when everyone is sitting next to strangers?[4] The obvious solution was to break the people into smaller groups. Small groups were not a new concept in church life, but here was the new spin: megachurches tried to divide people into groups by age. Large churches today now have youth groups, college ministries, seniors groups, etc., all of which are at least partially the result of being a large church . . . and the large church is partially a result of the invention of microphones and cars!

Now certainly if we look back into history, we can find churches that approximate the idea of the small groups, and churches that have large congregations. The large audiences of Jesus and Peter come to mind—as does Charles Spurgeon's church, whose building could accommodate almost 6,000 congregants. But historically, Spurgeon is a very rare example, and in fact his church is considered to be the precursor to the modern megachurch.

The significant thing we can learn from media ecology is that new technology presents people with a different set of choices than they had before. Technology still doesn't make anyone do anything, yet it seems that the presence of technology does urge societies in a certain direction, giving them benefits while also presenting them with new problems. Some of these trade-offs are not morally significant, but some do affect things as important as the life of the church. So how do these benefits and trade-offs occur?

Technological Means and Ends

One way to understand why technology always brings both benefits and trade-offs is to examine the connection between means and ends. If we think of technology as the means that we use to get to some end, then it's important to know whether or not the means affects the ends in some way.

To explain this, let's consider a nontechnological example. Imagine that you've been reading a long, complicated chapter on the philosophy of technology, and as you get toward the end you start to feel hungry. You want to find a means that will help you arrive at the end of being satiated. If there were no connection between means (food) and the end (satiation), then you could eat anything you wanted and always come to the same end. However, we know that the outcome will be different depending on whether you eat an apple or a Hostess Ding-Dong. Both food items will bring you to the same basic end (a full belly), but each means will also bring with them additional, different ends. The apple will make you feel full for longer, but the Ding-Dong will likely add to your waistline. The apple is biodegradable, while the Ding-Dong has a wrapper that will end up in a landfill somewhere.

This means that it's impossible to arrive at the simple end of being satiated without the means altering the end to some degree. Depending on which means of satiation you choose, you will arrive at a different, more complex end brought about by your food choice. Because of these, we say that ends and means are always connected.

This is fairly obvious when it comes to food, but it also applies when we use technology as a means to some end. If instrumentalism were true, then we should be able to switch out one technology for another and arrive at exactly the same end point. But just as switching the means from an apple to a Ding-Dong changes the ends at which we arrive, so also does changing from one technology to another.

Consider for a moment the means we use to travel from one location to another. In the early 1800s, the Christian missions movement exploded, sending missionaries from Europe and America all over Asia and Africa. In those days, missionaries would get to their destination on a ship whose voyage could take several weeks or even months. Today, newly minted missionaries hop on a plane, taking them from one continent to another in less than twenty-four hours. The starting and ending points are exactly the same, but the technology obviously transforms the experience. The most obvious difference between the ship and plane is the time it takes to travel, but even more significant is the meaning of that time. The voyage at sea often functioned as a slow, gradual transition from one culture to the next as missionaries spent time with fellow passengers from both their native culture and the one to which they were traveling. Today's missionaries don't have this built-in transition time and must adjust at warp speed when their plane touches foreign soil. On the other hand, faster travel means that today's missionaries are able to take more frequent furloughs and share more of what God is doing through them with the people who support them back home.

The point is that changing the means always alters the ends. As we transition from one technology to another, we never arrive at exactly the same end point. As Christians, we often say, "the means change, but the message stays the same." However, while it's true that the gospel message never changes, the means by which that message is communicated does, in fact, bring with it additional ends. Much of this is due to the fact that like all other things we create, our technology brings with it a set of values.

Technology and Values

When we talked about "cultivating the garden," we said that the act of making things always results in an embedding of values and meaning into that thing. We assign meaning to the things we make, and then when we use those things and perform cultural practices around them, they reflect back to us the values and meaning we assigned to them.

With some cultural goods like paintings, altars, and crucifixes, that meaning is explicit and by design. But with tools the values are more implicit, arising from a problem we believe we need to solve. Most tools reflect the importance assigned to them by their maker, and the problems the maker wants to solve. When we buy and use a tool, we are participating in solving what our culture considers to be a problem in need of a solution. For example, a culture that hunts game for food will tend to invent weapons, and it will value members of their society who can run fast. But a culture that plants crops for food will invent plows, and those people will value strong men and women. The hunter culture will then develop rituals around hunting and weapon-making that reinforce their importance for survival, while the farmers will create rituals around their seasonal planting.

This same kind of value-embedding takes place with modern technology as well. For example, when people created cars, one of the reasons they did so was that they valued traveling. Traveling by horse and wagon was slow, and traveling by train was limited to specific routes. The car would allow the speed of the train and the individual routes of a wagon. Although none of the early automobile innovators probably thought about it, the car now has embedded in it the value of allowing an individual to travel wherever, whenever.

The independence offered by the car, however, was not equally received in all cultures. In the late 1800s, people in the United States were already known for having a strong individualistic identity, and the automobile served to reinforce that value. Eventually, the car would become for Americans both a symbol of and a means to freedom. This was especially true for American teens, for whom the car was the tool that could take them from the world their parents controlled to a world where they were free to be and do whatever they pleased. In many parts of America today, the ritual of getting a car functions in the same way that becoming a hunter would have functioned for some Native Americans long ago.

If technological determinism were correct, we would assume that introducing a car into any culture would result in the same effect. But history tells a different story. When automobiles came to Europe, people there did not buy them at anywhere near the same rate as in America. The reasons for this are, of course, very complex, but it can be partially explained by the fact that Europeans have a different set of values, and so they treated the automobile differently. Perhaps because their cities were older and more historically rooted, the radical freedom offered by the automobile was not as attractive. This means that while technology contains in it the values of its makers, its users don't always react to those values in exactly the same way.

Another important factor to consider is that neither the makers nor early adopters of a tool know exactly what the tool will mean to the people who use it. For example, when mobile phones first appeared on the market, most of us bought them "only for emergencies." We thought it would be nice not to have to use a pay phone if we got stuck and needed help. We valued them for the safety and security they offered.

But the functionality of the phone is not limited to being able to make calls from anywhere; it also offers us the chance to be called from anywhere. The result is that as long as there are phones in our pockets, we are constantly connected to millions of other people who might call at any moment. Whoever we might happen to be with at the moment is just one of billions of people to whom we could be talking.

We bought our phones because we valued solving one problem (safety) without realizing that the phone also brings with it the value of constant connection. Then when we go for coffee with another person with our cell phone on, we are inadvertently agreeing to the value system issued by our cell phones, and this includes a value statement about the person in front of us. We are saying that we value not just his or her company but also the company of anyone else who might call.

If instrumentalism were true, then the presence of the cell phones shouldn't have an effect on our relationships, but experience tells us this is not true. On the other hand, if determinism were true, then we would have no choice as to whether or not we answer the call. Somewhere in between, we can say there is a tendency in the way that we will use any technology, and out of those tendencies a set of embedded values emerge.

Technology and the Flesh

Adding to this complexity is the fact that we live in a world where sin taints everything. What the Scriptures call our "flesh" is that part of us that is always bent toward self, at the expense of others and the exclusion of God. Our flesh, then, will always gravitate toward technology that favors the individual over the group. When a technology has the built-in value of personal choice and exclusion of others, our flesh will want to capitalize upon that value. This goes all the way back to Cain who used the technology of the city to insulate himself from God and his creation and serve his own selfish motives. If we combine what we know about the flesh with McLuhan's idea that technology "amplifies" an aspect of our humanity, we find that technology can amplify the "incurvature of the soul" about which Augustine wrote. Jesus warned us that when we attach a mouth to our heart, bad things often come out (Luke 6:47; cf. James 3). That sinfulness is amplified all the more when we attach something as powerful as the Internet to our hearts.

Our task as believers is to work against the tendencies built into our devices, and to in effect become a predator of the media in the ecosystem of our lives. Being a good predator means knowing one's prey well, and the more powerful the prey, the more careful we must be with it.

Today, successful technology companies are not those who build good products but those who can predict what the next tendency in technology will be. Likewise, Christians who live God-honoring lives in the digital world are those who can discern the tendencies built into all technology and then decide when those tendencies are in line with godly values, and when those tendencies are damaging to the soul. When we are aware of the tendencies and values inherent in our technology, we have the best chance of avoiding the negative trade-offs it brings and instead using the technology to serve God.

In the next chapter, we'll return to the Scriptures, where we'll find God beginning his program to redeem humanity; but we might be surprised to find that God sometimes takes advantage of the ways technology works within cultures to bring about redemptive ends. To illustrate this, I want to tell you a story about a curious new use of relatively old technology.

7

REDEMPTION

In the summer of 2009, Pastor Andy was diagnosed with Stage four colon cancer. He handled the news with grace, joking that his prognosis was "almost dead, but not quite," and that surgery was going to leave him with a semicolon, but underneath the humor our church wondered if we really were going to lose our beloved pastor of more than twenty years.

Immediately, the church body began praying for him, but one church member decided to do something special and a bit out of the ordinary. Chemotherapy can be grueling and exhausting, and those going through it often need more regular encouragement than the weekly "We've been praying for you" they hear every Sunday. So this church member bought a beeper, gave it to Andy, and then instructed everyone in the church to call it every time they petitioned God on Andy's behalf.

Andy came to church the next week with a huge smile on his face, and said that the beeper had been buzzing constantly through the day and even into the night. Sometimes the buzzing would go on for a minute or two when several people called it at once.

Soon, Andy started bringing the beeper everywhere, even into the waiting room at the hospital where he was being treated. He'd place the beeper out in plain view and start up a conversation with the other patients as it vibrated its way along the table. After a while, someone would finally say, "What's the deal with the beeper?" Andy would then tell about his illness, his congregation, and the faithfulness of his Savior. And faithful he was—in the spring of 2011, we found out that Andy was cancer free.

The reason I bring up Andy's beeper is not just that it's a great story, but because it demonstrates that sometimes even a normally annoying technology can function in a redemptive way. Using the ideas about technology from the last chapter, we could say that one of the values mediated by the beeper is its ability to distract a person from what they are doing to give them a message. The normal tendency of behavior built into the device is the need to carry it constantly and always submit to its distraction no matter where you are.

Used unreflectively, the beeps and dings from our devices pull us out of face-to-face contact with the people around us and into the world of the device. Yet, when we are aware of the tendencies and values of a technology, we have the opportunity to turn those values on their head. The buzzes from Andy's beeper distracted him (and the people in the waiting room) from the idea that there was no hope, that people didn't really care, and that God wasn't there with him. Normally, such a device would be annoying and even dehumanizing, but when someone applied a little creativity, the device was transformed into something that mediated an entirely different set of values.

And believe it or not, this kind of technology usage occasionally shows up in the Scriptures as God works his plan of redemption for humanity. We often think of God beginning his plan of redemption with Abraham in Genesis 12, but even before that God used technology in a few surprising ways to achieve a redemptive end. In prior chapters, we've seen that technology can serve both to reflect the creativity of God and rebel against him. In this chapter, we'll see a third aspect of technology—sometimes God uses the tendencies and value systems inherent in technology to move along his redemptive purposes. There are dozens of stories that we simply don't have room to discuss (David's adoption of Hittite iron-smelting tools comes to mind), so we will limit our discussion to three familiar episodes: Noah's ark, the Tower of Babel, and the giving of the Law to Moses.

Blueprints

Back in the garden, we saw God graciously upgrade Adam and Eve's first act of technological creation by remaking their clothing with better materials. Obviously, the clothing could not fully restore them to their pre-fall state, but it did protect them from the harsh new world they were about to experience. In this sense, the tool of clothing offered Adam and Eve a form of redemption, albeit a temporary one. As we step out of the garden, we'll see that this was not the only time God will choose to use technology in his redemptive work.

The first is the story of Noah's ark, a story usually relegated to teaching children about animals, rainbows, and God's graciousness. Biblical scholars also find other important themes and messages, but rarely if ever do we read Noah's story with technology in mind. And yet Noah's ark-building project lines up quite well with our definition of technology as "the human activity of using tools to transform God's creation for practical ends."

Interestingly, the story of Noah in Genesis 5 begins with a restatement of the fact that God created male and female humans in his image and likeness. Then the Scripture goes further, saying that Adam fathered children in his image and likeness. The idea is that even in this sin-cursed world where brothers kill one another, God's image—and the creativity therein—is still being passed down from generation to generation.

At the end of chapter 5, we read that a man named Lamech named his child Noah and says that he hopes Noah will be able to "provide comfort" to those suffering from the effects of the fall (verse 29). Lamech doesn't mention sin directly, but he does say that he hopes Noah will relieve God's curse on the ground and the "painful toil of our hands" (Gen. 5:28). Lamech seems to view his son as a kind of savior from the curse of the fall and, as we all know, Noah was a kind of deliverer—just not exactly the kind for which his father had hoped.

After the birth of Noah in Genesis 5, Genesis 6 makes it clear that the other families of the earth had become terribly wicked. Their wickedness grieved God so deeply that he wanted to destroy every human on earth. God is so incensed with their sin that he decided to destroy them with the creation they were designed to cultivate and keep: "Behold! I will destroy them with the earth" (Gen. 6:13).

Thankfully, Noah found favor in the eyes of God; and God decided that even in his act of destruction, he would provide a way to save the human race. What comes next in the story is so familiar to us that it's difficult to step back and see how unexpected God's plan was. Keep in mind that this is the same God who parted the Red Sea for the Israelites, so he certainly could have supernaturally prevented the waters from reaching Noah. He could have sent the Angel of Death to every house but Noah's or performed any number of other miracles. But for some reason, God chose to destroy humanity in a supernatural torrent of floodwaters, and then save humanity using a technology he designed himself. In the following verses, God actually gives Noah the exact blueprints for the tool he is to build, including precise measurements and materials:

> Make yourself an ark of gopher wood. Make rooms in the ark, and cover it inside and out with pitch. This is how you are to make it: the length of the ark 300 cubits, its breadth 50 cubits, and its height 30 cubits. Make a roof for the ark, and finish it to a cubit above, and set the door of the ark in its side. Make it with lower, second, and third decks. (Gen. 6:14–16)

Again, as one of the most well-known stories of the Bible, none of this feels out of the ordinary. But what's happening is not too far removed from a science fiction movie, the kind where a kid finds the blueprints to an alien technology that can save the world. But there's no alien here and no

Hollywood special effects—this is the God of the universe telling Noah what kind of sealer to use on his boat. In what *should* come as a major surprise to us, it is through this human-made, God-designed ark—a technology created from the raw material of the earth—that humanity finds salvation from the floodwaters of God's wrath. God certainly didn't need the ark to save Noah and his family, but for some reason it was important for Noah to *make* it. Again we see that the word "make" (the same one used to describe Adam and Eve's clothing) shows up repeatedly in this chapter, and the chapter ends with the words, "Noah *made* all that God had commanded" (Gen. 6:22).

When the floodwaters receded and Noah stepped out of the boat, it appeared that the human race would get a fresh start. God renewed his commands to be fruitful and multiply, and put in place the seeds of a formal government structure (Gen. 9:6) in hopes of preventing the kind of evil that was washed away in the great flood. Noah then planted a vineyard (Gen. 9:20), recalling images of the Garden of Eden and symbolizing a fresh start for humanity.

But even with this rebooting of the human race, Noah's ark did not eradicate the virus of human sin. Sin had infected those caught in the floodwaters as well as the passengers of the ark. Even the ship's captain, the hoped-for savior Noah, was hopelessly enslaved to sin. Almost immediately, we find that Noah's sons tainted the fruits of his vineyard; and instead of cultivating and keeping it for God's glory, they perverted it for their own sinful lusts (Gen. 9:21–24).

By the end of the story, it's clear that Noah and his ark didn't offer humanity the salvation for which Lamech had hoped. Of course, we wouldn't expect technology to save us, yet this story seems to tell us that technology has redemptive capacity. It can offer us relief from suffering and, in some cases, help us avoid death.

Like the clothing God made in Eden, the ark temporarily protected humanity from some of the curses of the fall. But God didn't just use the ark to relieve physical ailments, he also used it to nurse along the human race, protecting them from judgment and taking the first steps in securing their redemption. So why did God use a technology of his own design rather than some other supernatural means as part of his redemptive strategy?

In the previous chapter, one of the things we learned about technology is that the means (the tool) and ends (the outcome) are always connected. God certainly knows this as well, which means that his choice of means is always deliberate and meaningful. Perhaps God is telling us that he values not just humanity but also the creations of humanity. The use of the ark seems to indicate that the physical world—and what we make with it—is so important to God that he graciously chooses to use what we make in his plan of redemption. He doesn't *need* to use what we make, but apparently it pleases him to do so.

Indeed, many people have noticed the parallels between Noah and his ark and Jesus and the cross. Both Noah and Jesus were righteous men who delivered the human race by means of wooden tools. Of course, the tools themselves are powerless to save us. They are not magical, and they have no command over sin and death. Yet God has seen fit to use them to bring about his redemptive purposes.

I think this should encourage us that for all the trade-offs and unintended consequences that technology brings, we too can employ technology for redemptive ends. Digging wells for clean water, offering medicine to the sick, and even sending encouraging emails work against the sin that entered the world at the fall. And when we use technology in service of the mission of the Church to make disciples, we are following God's lead in using technology as a part of his redemptive plans.

Yet we must also be careful to affirm that the redemptive capacity of technology is limited and temporary. Advances in technology can give us the illusion that it might someday overcome death, but this is a tragic and distracting lie. Clean water and ample medicine can only hold off death for so long—eventually death will find us all. Instead, we should view the redemptive capacities of technology as a temporary means of keeping humanity going while God does his work. He used the ark to keep humanity going long enough to save us, and we too can think of technology as a way of keeping humans alive while God does his work in and through us.

When we dig wells for the thirsty and bring food to the hungry, these acts temporarily overcome the curse of the fall; at the same time, they allow space for God's program to continue. God, of course, doesn't need our tools to accomplish his plans, but in his wisdom he has chosen to use them. In the next story, however, we'll see that God doesn't just work through technology—sometimes he works against it.

Social Networking

In the last few years, we've all seen how powerful social networking technology can be to connect people, start movements, and transmit information. Facebook, Twitter, and the rest have transformed the way we view information, friendships, and what is important to us. They've also reinforced the kind of empowerment that comes when like-minded individuals find each other and work together to accomplish a shared goal. In recent years, groups of people have banded together online to do noble things like raise money for orphanages. Some have done ignoble things, like taunting fellow classmates, and others have done silly things, like getting Betty White on Saturday Night Live.[1] In each case, social networking technology amplified the inherent power of a group of people united around a common mission.

But long before Facebook existed, the story of the Tower of Babel in Genesis tells us quite a bit about what happens when people join together around a technology. In Genesis 11, we find the human race again rejecting God's plans for them in favor of technological achievement. Rather than using their creative powers to honor God as Noah did, the people of Babel wanted to bring glory to themselves. Rather than live in dependence upon God (as Abraham will in the coming chapters), they tried to achieve complete autonomy from him. Like Cain, the people of Babel saw technology as the means by which they could overcome the limits of a sinful world and remain independent of God. When God created the garden, he put humankind in it to reflect his image. At Babel, we find humans creating a city as their anti-garden and a tower as an image to themselves.

Obviously this was of great concern to God who worried that "nothing that they propose to do will now be impossible for them" (Gen. 11:6). Initially it seems like God was concerned that the people of Babel were growing too powerful and that their creation would enable them to outstrip his control. But the word usually translated "do" in the sentence—"nothing which they purpose to do"—is the same Hebrew word as the one for "make" that we've seen throughout the first few chapters of Genesis. Again, God's concern is that the people of Babel were abusing their creative powers to derail his design for humanity. The tower was an idol distracting them from the command to spread out and fill the earth.

As with the story of Noah, the ending of the story is so familiar to us that it doesn't seem terribly surprising. But if we take a moment to think about it from a fresh perspective, God could have simply leveled their tower and crushed the walls of their city as he did with Jericho. Instead, however, he chose to attack something more fundamental to their lives—their language. As we saw in chapter 3, language is something that we create not only to communicate information but also to establish a sense of identity and inform the way we see the world. Many anthropologists say that if you truly want to learn about a people group, you need only to learn their language and it will tell you all you need to know. So by confusing their languages, God was essentially reprogramming their sense of self, their relational connections, and how they viewed the world.

Interestingly, language is just as important to us today as it was for the people of Babel. We don't depend on a specific universal language, but the technology we use to transmit ideas has become essential to our way of life. One way to see the depth of our dependence on communication technology is to watch how our movie villains have evolved in recent decades. In the 1970s and 1980s, action movie bad guys were scary Russians threatening to release nuclear bombs. In the 1990s and early 2000s, the villains morphed into Arabs committing acts of terrorism. But in many of today's movies, the villains are hackers who threaten to destroy our computer networks, take down the banking system, and reset our entire way of life.

What God did to the people of Babel was not too far from these technology-inspired thrillers. By reprogramming the fundamental technology of the human race—language—God disrupted their entire way of life. Confusion, however, was not God's ultimate goal; instead, he was forcing the people to fulfill the commandment to fill the earth. Again, God might have chosen any means of doing this, but he saw fit to use the technology of language as the means of scattering people. The people who deeply trusted technology to give them security and meaning had those very things stripped away from them by technological change. Notice that God was able to change their behavior, but he didn't have to take away their free will or destroy their creation to do so. All he had was to introduce technological change.

Technological change doesn't force anyone to do something, but it does change the choices a person can make. By taking away their shared language, God took away the choice to work against him. At the same time, new languages presented the people with a new set of choices as to how they would reorganize.

I think there are three important things we should notice in the story of the Tower of Babel. The first is that God is again using technology to effect his plan to restore humanity to the purpose for which he created them. Through the Scriptures God often works through people, yet sometimes he takes decisive action and performs supernatural acts. In the case of the ark, God used technology to protect humanity. But in the confusion of languages at Babel, God worked against the values of technology. A universal language has the built-in value of connecting a people with a single identity, and God chose to work against that value by breaking up their linguistic ties.

The second important truth in this story is that technology cannot be separated from the social world. Today much of our technology is personalized and focused on the individual's preferences, but in reality every technological choice we make takes place within the context of our culture and community. Moreover, technology, which is designed to be socially oriented, is particularly powerful in motivating large groups of people to do things. People often do things in groups that they would not do as individuals, and technology only reinforces this social dynamic. The Tower of Babel should remind us that social networks are not just toys—they are part of the most powerful technology in the world.

Finally, what happened at Babel illustrates that when a technological change happens within a culture, that change in technology results in a change in the culture. Technology does not *make* people do anything, but it does alter the choices people have in front of them. God didn't force the Babelites to move, but by changing their communication technology, he made it extremely difficult for them to choose to stay put.

Even today, technological change often results in a realignment of a society. When we introduce technological change in our families, jobs, or churches, we too will face a different set of choices, limitations, and abilities. Each new tool has a series of strengths and weaknesses and a unique set of values, and these factors work in concert to shape our world and influence our choices. Perhaps no story illustrates this better than the exodus.

Tablet Revolution

When Apple released its first generation iPad, some technology observers thought it was going to "change everything"—or at the very least change the way we read books and magazines. Others, however, were content to sit back and make jokes, comparing Steve Job's tablet to the tablets Moses brought down from Mount Sinai. All joking aside, what God did in calling the Hebrew people out of Egypt, bringing them into Canaan, and providing them a set of written instructions on how to live was nothing short of a cultural revolution. There is enormous theological significance to the role of Israel in God's redemptive plan, and we cannot possibly do justice to all of it here. But we will spend a few pages considering the small but significant role that technology and media played in the identity of Israel.

Let's first take a broad look at the content of the Law that God gave Moses in the books of Exodus, Leviticus, Numbers, and Deuteronomy. First, there are hundreds of detailed laws covering ethical and social conduct such as how to marry, how to handle infidelity, how to parent children, how to handle land disputes, and so on. Mixed in with these are laws that set up a legal and governmental structure for the people who would someday become a nation.

In addition to these social and legal laws, God did something he hadn't done since the days of Noah—he handed Moses a set of blueprints for an ark. But this ark—the ark of the covenant—wasn't designed to carry people. Instead it carried the signs of God's faithfulness to his people. In addition to the plans for the ark, Moses wrote down God's specifications for the tabernacle and every element of worship inside it, from the clothing worn by the priests to the altars on which they would offer him sacrifices. God planned out everything in meticulous detail, down to kinds of threads, metals, stones, and other materials the Israelites were to use for each element. In addition, God told the Israelites how they were to use each piece of the tabernacle and the order in which they were to use them. If a priest made a single mistake, the penalty was immediate death.

These details are included in what is probably one of the longest and least-read divisions of the Bible. This is because this part of the Bible contains two things people don't generally like to read: genealogies and measurements. While it is admittedly not a terribly entertaining read, this section of the Bible is amazing for one simple reason: there in the Middle Eastern desert, God took a group of slaves and gave them a set of objects, images, rituals, and language that would transform them into an entirely new culture, distinct from everyone around them. He handed them detailed descriptions of everyday cultural goods and artifacts as well as the practices and rituals they were to perform with them. God wanted his people to be "holy" or "set apart," and one of the best ways to do this was to give them an entirely new set of objects and rituals designed to communicate their identity as the people of God with the values of their Creator.

As we saw with Adam and Eve and Noah, it's not out of the ordinary for God to step in and help people with their tools, but here God takes it to another level by showing the Hebrews exactly how he wanted them to live every aspect of their lives. As New Testament Christians, we rightly rejoice in the fact that Jesus came to fulfill the Law and, as Paul reminds us, "Christ is the end of the law for anyone who believes" (Rom. 10:4). However, it is worth our time to take a second look at elements of culture that God created for Israel, because in them we can find some important principles for today's technology.

It Is Written

One of the most important aspects of the entire Law of Israel is simply that it was written down. Most Christian scholars believe that Moses and the Israelites crossed the Red Sea around 1444 B.C., meaning that God would have carved out the first set of stone tablets around that time, and Moses would have written the Law after that.

What is fascinating about this is that when God wrote the Ten Commandments on stone tablets, alphabetical writing was still a bleeding edge technology. People had been speaking and using language since the days of Adam, but in Moses' day writing itself was still a fairly new concept. At some point in history, humans started creating cave art, and gradually those drawings morphed into the kind of hieroglyphics that we see in ancient Egyptian tombs. Those hieroglyphics are often called pictograms because each drawing represents a word or a concept. Instead of the twenty-six characters that we have in our alphabet, a pictographic language can have thousands and thousands of symbols. This meant that hieroglyphics were a new exciting way to share stories, but they weren't terribly efficient at doing so.

After a few centuries of using pictograms, someone decided that instead of using symbols to represent an idea or an object, symbols could be created to represent sounds. This was called a phonetic (sound-based) alphabet, and it is the basis of the alphabet we use today. Scholars debate the exact time frame and location of the first phonetic alphabet, but everyone agrees that it originated in the region of Canaan, Sinai, or Egypt between the nineteenth and fifteenth centuries B.C.

The importance of these dates is that, during this time, the descendants of Jacob and Joseph were enslaved in Egypt. This means that the Hebrews were effectively living in the Silicon Valley of their day, watching the first major communication revolution. Although they didn't create the first alphabet, early forms of Hebrew are directly related to those first alphabets.

While it's certainly interesting to know that God used the high-tech equipment of that day to communicate to the Israelites, there is additional significance to the technology of writing itself. In fact, the technology of writing is one of the most powerful transformative agents one can introduce into a culture.

Before writing, the only place to store information and ideas was in a person's mind. If you wanted to know something, the only way to get that information was to ask another human being. And if you wanted to get the most accurate data, you would naturally go see the oldest people in town, since it would be the elder of the community who would have accumulated the most information. In oral societies, before writing was invented, young people automatically looked up to their elders since they were the best and only source of knowledge.

Writing turned this social arrangement on its head because, for the first time, writing allowed knowledge to reside outside the human mind. Writing is so ancient that we no longer see it as a technology, but it was perhaps the most transformative of all the "extensions of man" because it was the first to extend the mind. Today, storing data outside our minds is an everyday occurrence as we store almost all of our knowledge on paper or computers. We jot down to-do lists and keep our spending on spreadsheets, but before writing none of this was possible. Any information that wasn't stored in the mind of a living person was inaccessible, and if a person died without passing on this knowledge, the knowledge, too, would die.

The technology of writing meant that any person who could read had access to information that would normally take a lifetime to accumulate. No matter how young or old a person was, the one who could acquire the skill of decoding letters no longer needed other human beings to gain knowledge. A young person who had been educated could become a respected leader of the people.

And this is just what happened with the transition in leadership from Moses to Joshua. God called Moses to lead the Israelites out of Egypt when he was eighty years old, and Moses died when he was approximately 120. But Joshua was chosen to lead the people at a much younger age without experiencing all that Moses had seen of God.

The Bible tells us that God chose Joshua because of the faith he demonstrated when he trusted that God would give his people victory over the Canaanites. When Moses died, the technology of writing allowed Joshua to have access to Moses' knowledge of God and the commandments he laid out for Israel. Faith and righteousness were still requirements for spiritual leadership, but writing meant that age was no longer necessary.

The technology of writing also brought with it a sense of permanence and authority. Speech is fluid and when we transfer ideas from one person to another, we tend to introduce small changes over time. If you've ever played the game "Telephone," you know how quickly speech gets transformed when it travels from person to person. In contrast, the technology of writing values exactness and precision. By choosing this technology, God was communicating that his Law did not contain optional truths or malleable commands. His Law was literally set in stone.

In the early days of writing, paper and ink were incredibly expensive. This meant that people could only afford to write down what was of the highest importance to them. Unlike our throwaway to-do lists, virtually everything written down was vital. This meant that when people invoked the words "It is written," they were appealing to the authority of the medium. After all, it wouldn't be written if it weren't important.

So God chose a medium of communication that was not only cutting edge for the time but also reinforced the message of that Law. In creating the culture of the people of Israel, God was giving the world his final, authoritative, and unchanging Law. And he chose a technological medium that reinforced those values.

God, in his infinite wisdom, orchestrated the timing of the exodus so it would line up with the availability of the technology of writing. When we fast-forward to the time of Jesus' arrival, we find that God again timed it to coincide with another set of technological developments. In the centuries leading up to Jesus' birth, two major technologies had spread across the Greco-Roman world enabling the gospel to spread like a virus on the Internet. The first was the availability of the Greek language. When Alexander the Great conquered most of the known world, everyone in his kingdom learned Greek. For the first time since Babel, there was a common language among the peoples of the earth. This time, God employed that common language as the means of transmitting the gospel to Judea, Samaria, and the ends of the earth. But for Paul and company to get to the ends of the earth, they needed a second technology—roads. In the centuries after Alexander's conquest, the Romans built roads between every major city, enabling those first missionaries to take the good news just about anywhere.

God, then, seems to always be at the forefront of technological usage. There is no "wait-and-see" policy—instead God is always working through the tools of the day as he accomplishes his redemptive program. However, we ought not to conclude from God that he doesn't care about which tools we use. In fact, in the words of the Law, we find that God did not limit his outlook to the medium of writing. He also had his eye on another powerful medium of communication and culture—the image.

The Importance of Images

When we think of the Old Testament world, we don't usually think of magazines, billboards, flat screen TVs, and all the other images we see every day. And yet, the Ten Commandments make a special point to address these. Let's read the first two commandments:

1. You shall have no other gods before me.
2. You shall not make for yourself a carved image. . . . You shall not bow down to them or serve them.[2]

The first commandment is the central defining difference of Israel from all cultures that surrounded it. The Hebrews were not to treat Yahweh as the highest god among the pantheon of goddesses and goddesses. Instead they were to be monotheists, with the identity of a nation that worshipped Yahweh, the one true God, and Yahweh alone.

Then the very next commandment concerns the word that keeps popping up in our study of media and technology—"make." Before God said anything about murdering, stealing, or coveting, he gave the people of Israel guidelines referring back to the creation mandate from Genesis 1 and 2. The Hebrews were not free to approach God however they pleased, through whatever means they might find enlightening, fun, or interesting. Instead God comes out of the gate with explicit commands on the relationship between their making and their worship.

When we look back at the ethical systems of other cultures around this time, many of them have commands that are reminiscent of the other commandments like "Thou shalt not murder" and "Thou shalt not steal." But these first two commandments are completely unique to anything found in the ancient world. No other ancient rule set commanded monotheism, and no other system puts such a high importance on the tools and objects used for worship. Neil Postman (who was himself of Jewish descent) noted this difference when he wrote, "It is a strange injunction to include as part of an ethical system [instructions on how they were to symbolize, or not symbolize, their experience] *unless its author assumed a connection between forms of human communication and the quality of a culture.*"[3] An Israelite might have said, "What difference does it make if I create an idol to represent God, if I'm still worshipping Yahweh?" But in the second commandment, God is telling Israel that the images, forms, and tools through which we approach him do, in fact, matter to him.

Although God is restricting the use of a particular medium—carved images—he does so for a very important reason. It's not that God thinks images themselves are inherently evil. It's because he recognizes that tools of technology never function as neutral, inert instruments. Instead the tools we use always bring with them values that shape the culture that uses them. If God had allowed the Israelites to make images of him, it might have appeared that he was like every other god, or a god among gods. Instead, by forbidding images of himself, God reinforced his identity as wholly other.

He is not an idol among idols or an image among images—he is the one
true God. Therefore, God decreed that the people of Israel were to approach
him exclusively through the names, metaphors, and ideas found in the permanent, authoritative words of Scripture. The medium was the message.

In our quick skim of the Old Testament, we have passed over many
important chapters in the redemptive story. But it has become increasingly
clear that God has chosen technology and culture to play a role in his plan.
God has indicated that the things we make—technology included—matter
to him, and that he can operate both through and against them. He has
also demonstrated that the mediums we use to communicate, worship, and
approach him are incredibly important. Throughout the Old Testament,
there are echoes and hints that one day God will be *im*mediate, but until
that day we need to spend time more fully exploring how technological
mediums work, and to do so I am forced to tell you about a time when I
received a B in seminary.

MEDIUMS

I only received two B's in seminary, and I'm a little embarrassed to admit that one of those was in a class on evangelism. The good news is that I learned an important lesson about technology, which I attribute to a hilarious South American professor named Oscar Lopez.

Every professor at DTS dresses professionally, but Dr. Lopez always takes it up a notch and wears a suit with a very colorful tie. One day, he came to class dressed nicely as usual and said that he was going to teach about how nonverbal communication could impact our evangelism efforts. He began by making a joke about his deep Spanish accent, but as he transitioned into teaching about communication theory, he did something that was unusual for him—he took off his suit coat and put it over the back of his chair. As he continued, he reached up to his neck and slowly pulled down on his bright red tie. It's pretty common for people to loosen their tie in the Texas heat, but strangely Dr. Lopez kept pulling on it until it came completely off, at which point he draped the tie over his suit coat.

Then he really surprised everyone when he started unbuttoning his dress shirt revealing his white sleeveless shirt underneath. He kept on speaking as if this were perfectly normal, but my classmates started looking around at each other and wondering what in the world was happening. After he took his dress shirt completely off, he added it to the pile of clothes on his chair and asked us, "Do you know why I wear a suit and tie to class every day?"

The room was silent. No one knew what to say.

After a few moments, Dr. Lopez said, "Because if I came into class looking like this, you'd think I was a gardener!"

Now Dr. Lopez is a respected professor and someone to whom we wanted to give our highest respect. None of us wanted to laugh at a joke with racial undertones, but here in front of us was an older man of Latino descent wearing a white sleeveless undershirt, which, in the South, is the stereotypical dress code for a person who works outdoors. Dr. Lopez, of course, found our squeamishness hilarious, and after letting the awkwardness linger for several very long seconds, he burst into laughter, saying, "You seminary students are so serious!"

He then put his shirt back on and started to recite some of the ideas that we've all heard about the art of speaking, such as, "Ninety percent of communication is tone of voice." But he went on to say that it's not just tone of voice that affects how people interpret what we say. A variety of other factors affect communication, including accent, gender, race, etc. In a sense, any time we're speaking to someone, we are taking the ideas in our minds and wrapping them in elements of who we are as a person. We then hand that entire package to the person listening, and their reaction is composed of what they think of both the words and the packaging.

Though we don't always notice it, we constantly make judgments about the words people say based on nonverbal factors of the speaker. For example, Americans often assume a speaker with a British accent is more refined and intelligent than an American speaker. When men listen to women, they tend to pay more attention to attractive women, but conversely often take the opinions of unattractive women more seriously. When we see a speaker for the first time, we may immediately begin forming opinions about him or her that have as much to do with the speaker's confidence and appearance as content. In most cases, wearing a suit to a job interview drastically increases your chances of landing the job. Then again, that same suit might communicate a kind of stuffiness to another group of people.

We could go on and on making these kinds of observations, but the general point is that communication is about more than just words. Words don't come without packaging and that packaging always brings with it its own message. But this packaging is not limited to aspects of our personal identity such as our gender, accent, and choice of clothing. Today, communication technologies are also kinds of packaging and they, too, have their own messages and impact.

What Is a Medium?

When we move from communicating in person to communicating through technological means, we are, in effect, rewrapping our words in a new set of packaging. Instead of wrapping our words in elements of our identity, we wrap them with the identity, values, and meaning inherent in the particular technology we choose.

We call those packages—whether it is an email, a handwritten note, a phone call, a Facebook wall post, or any other tool we use to communicate—*mediums*.[1] The *message* is the content we transmit from our minds to our audience, while everything that surrounds those words can be considered a *medium*.

When God communicated the *message* of the Law, he did so conscious not just of his words but also of the *medium* through which those words came. We, too, need to become aware of how mediums work, and we will say that they do at least three things: they communicate meaning, they create new cultures, and they shape our thinking patterns.

Mediums Communicate Meaning

I recently signed up for two new online services as part of my job as a web developer. When I paid for the first service, the company immediately emailed a receipt to me, and then followed that up with an email thanking me for my business. When I signed up for the second service, they too sent me a receipt but a few days later I found a handwritten thank-you note from them in the mail. I double-checked it, thinking it might be a printed letter designed to look handwritten, but it turned out to be the real thing. The thank-you email from the first company and the thank-you letter from the second contained almost identical wording, but I immediately found myself thinking more highly of the second. The content of both messages was exactly the same, but the message I received was quite different, and this difference was solely due to the medium. Both companies said the words, "Thank you," but the words on ink and paper seemed more genuine and meaningful than those on a screen.

Of course, differences between mediums are not quite as dramatic as this example, but every medium brings with it some kind of meaning that is tied to its functionality. To help expose these meanings, we will look at tendencies hidden in the way we use various communication mediums: formality, difficulty, and speed.

Formality. The difference between a phone call and a text message is not just about hearing a voice versus reading a screen. Each technology also encourages a different kind of social interaction. First, a phone call has to be accepted while a text message comes in automatically. In addition, both parties can be heard simultaneously in a phone call, while each text message is only one way. The phone call has a clear beginning and end, while each text message just happens. Because of these technical differences, we usually begin a phone call with a greeting like, "Hello, how are you?" and end it with a closing like, "Talk to you later."[2] Text messages don't require us to do either of these things because there is no defined beginning or ending to a text message.

For example, let's imagine my friend and I are going to meet for a movie, and I need to tell him the time and place. If I send him a text message, it will say, "John Dyer: 9 pm at Cinemark." However, if I call him, he will see my name on his phone, answer it, and say, "Hey John, what time is the movie?"

and I will respond with, "9 pm at Cinemark." Notice that the phone call tends to require that we add a layer of interaction (a greeting) before the exchange of information. The further back we go technologically, the more layers of interaction were required. Back when phones didn't identify who was calling, we would begin a phone call with, "Hello, who is this?" and then respond with, "Hey, this is John calling about the movie." Here we've added a layer of identification before we get to the greeting and finally to the information, "Oh, hey John. So what time is the movie?"

If we go back a few more decades to when everyone in a household shared the same phone, then we would add another layer of conversation. If my friend's wife answered their phone, I would first ask to speak to him before we could address the issue of movie times. Going back even further, there was a time when phones didn't have phone numbers that automatically connected them. Instead, you'd have to first speak to an operator and ask him or her to connect you to the phone in your friend's house. Then you could speak to his wife and ask her to let you speak to him, and then you could— finally!—tell him what time the movie was playing.

These examples tell us something very simple, and yet very important, about mediums. In general, more advanced communication technology requires fewer steps and, therefore, there are fewer social conventions required for its use. When there are more built-in social conventions around using a medium, we tend to treat it more formally and what we communicate tends to be more significant (as in writing a letter). Conversely, when a newer technology removes the need for these social conventions, it also removes the sense of formality (as in a text message).

In the era before electronic communication, the only way to communicate with another person was to see the person face-to-face, or send a handwritten note (which required pen and paper, an envelope, an address, and a stamp). Electronic media allows us to connect with anyone, anywhere, anytime, wearing anything or nothing at all. And these differences in formality tend to influence what we talk about together. Newer mediums remove formality and make things easier . . . which leads to our next observation.

Difficulty. The act of getting dressed and traveling to see a friend and the act of physically carrying a letter to a mailbox are both more difficult than a quick text message or email that can be sent immediately with much less effort. This difference in difficulty is part of the reason older mediums tend to communicate a deeper sense of meaning and value than newer mediums do. For example, the handwritten note from the second company in the example above seemed more meaningful to me in part because I knew it took more effort for them to do. Similarly, if a girl tells her boyfriend, "I think we should date other people," he will perceive those words differently if she says them in person, via a letter, or via text message. He will likely be disappointed by the message no matter how she delivers it, but since the text message requires the least amount of effort, it will probably hurt the most.

When we look around at other social conventions, we find that we almost always use older cultural goods when we want to signify that something is important. Couples getting married wear older styles of clothing—tuxedos and long, beautiful gowns—to make the statement that this is a significant event. If a couple wants to make a date special, they forgo driving their car around downtown in favor of hiring a horse and buggy to take them on that same path. The older technology makes the event seem more significant. Again, we see that technology as an element of culture is always mediating to us meaning, value, and identity.

Going back to our communication tools, we often find that the relative difficulty and time it takes to use a medium communicates the significance of the message. For example, after I applied for a job at a church, the pastor asked me to go to lunch. As we sat together he told me how much he valued me, but that I was not right for the job. He was right, and it hurt to hear, but the amount of time and effort he took to communicate the painful truth made the wound a little less severe. He could have communicated using dozens of easier, faster tools; but he used the slowest, most meaningful medium—a face-to-face encounter—and that choice communicated that he did, in fact, value me as a person.

The range in difficulty from newer to older mediums can also account for many communication problems. When a medium is more difficult or expensive to use, we tend to put more thought into our words. Conversely, the easier a medium is to use and the less costly it is to us, we are more likely to use it without much thought. Part of the reason for this is that when a medium is easier to use, it is because that medium is doing most of the communication for us. In a handwritten note, the person on the other end can see something of us—our handwriting and our mistakes—but in an email only the letters can be seen as the computer renders them. In other words, the older medium has more of you and less of the machine while the newer medium is more machine and less you.

This relative difference in humanity often accounts for some of the communication problems we have in the digital age. Emails intended to be lighthearted can be interpreted as mean-spirited simply because the email lacks tone of voice, body language, or even difference in pen strokes that cue a person into the playfulness of the message. Certainly, easier to use and less costly mediums bring incredible advantages and open up massive new avenues of personal connection. But we must keep in mind that anytime we communicate something of significance through a medium that is easy to use, we run the risk of our audience misinterpreting it since it is more machine than human. And this brings us to a third difference in electronic media: speed.

Speed. The ease and speed of newer mediums also enables us to send messages that we would not have sent given more time for reflection. On one particular occasion, when I heard about how a business transaction was handled, I became very frustrated and quickly fired off an angry email to everyone involved. Later, when I cooled down, I had to go back and apologize to everyone for some of the things I said in that email. Had this same set of circumstances happened in a world without email, the time it would take to prepare handwritten, individually stamped letters for all of those people might have allowed me to cool down before I sent my rash messages.

Apparently this is so common that Google added a feature to its Gmail product called "Mail Goggles" that attempts to help people avoid sending middle-of-the-night emails that they might later regret. Since people are often drunk or otherwise emotionally compromised in the wee hours of the night, Mail Goggles requires users to solve several math problems before it will allow them to send those late-night messages. The idea is to slow down the immediacy of email and give people a little more time to consider what they are sending.

But using a newer, faster medium doesn't always communicate that the message is less significant. In certain cases, the speed of a newer medium heightens the significance of a message. For example, if a person attending a sporting event sends the score of a game to another person not in attendance, that message will obviously be more significant if it is sent in real time with a text than if it were sent via regular mail arriving days later. If a college admissions counselor sends a prospective student a text telling her that she's been accepted to the university, the use of texting might communicate that the university understands her generation and how they prefer to communicate.

It's important to note that depending on a person's age and familiarity with a medium, he or she might not agree with what I've just said about formality, difficulty, and speed; and this brings up a second and perhaps even more important truth about mediums. Mediums not only communicate meaning, they also tend to create, divide, and reshape cultures.

Mediums Create Culture (and Cultural Divides)

Back in chapter 1, Douglas Adams was quoted as saying that technology can be divided into three categories: (1) everything before you were born is just "stuff," (2) everything invented between birth and the age of thirty is wonderful, and (3) everything invented after you turn thirty will bring about the death of society. Why is it that people sometimes treat technology this way? Part of the reason is that language and culture are bound together very tightly, and any change in the way we communicate results in a change to our culture and way of life. People over thirty have spent their entire lives learning one pattern of communication, and when new communication tools come along, they disrupt these patterns.

Imagine for example that Americans suddenly decided to replace shaking hands with bowing as the way to greet one another. For most adults bowing would feel strange, different, and unnatural. It might take years for bowing to take hold and feel familiar, and even then some people just wouldn't like the change. However, if we taught our kids to bow from birth, it would never feel unnatural to them. They wouldn't have experienced "handshake culture," so they would only encounter handshaking in history books or quaint small towns.

The result would be two groups of people: those raised with handshakes for whom bowing feels strange, and those raised with bowing for whom bowing is completely natural. The two mediums of greeting will be interpreted and used differently depending on who is using them.

Something similar to my handshaking/bowing scenario happens when families immigrate to another country. One of my neighbors emigrated from an Eastern European country to start a family with his wife in America. His English is very good, yet for him it is—and always will be—a second language. However, his kids are native English speakers, and all they've ever known is American culture. One of his kids is now a teenager wanting to find ways to be independent from his parents, so he has decided to reject everything about his parents' home country, including the native language. This difference in language has effectively created two distinct cultures in their home and a chasm between parent and child.

Today, this kind of cultural divide isn't just happening in families who immigrate to a country with a different language. It also happens whenever new communication mediums come on the market and find their way into families. Younger people tend to figure out new media more quickly than their parents, and we often say that they are more "tech savvy" than older people. But what's really happening is that the new medium feels like a foreign language to an adult, but for the younger person it's just the way things are. The adult approaches new mediums the same way my neighbor approaches English—he can learn it, but he will never be a "native" speaker.

This doesn't mean that all older people are technologically inept, or that all younger people are automatically able to use any new technology. In general it does mean that when a person encounters a technology later in life, he or she will tend to use it with a "think accent," showing their ease with older mediums. Educator Marc Prensky coined the terms "digital natives" and "digital immigrants" to describe this divide.[3] Digital natives grow up with technology, and the use of technology becomes engrained in the way these individuals think and go about life. But digital immigrants are always learning and playing catch-up, like an adult learning a second language.

This means that right now in households all over the globe there are people from several different cultures. Depending on when they first used various communication technologies, those mediums will hold different meanings for them. For example, today's teenagers tend to be much more comfortable with texting than their parents. They send and receive thousands of messages per month and they do so with a speed that very few parents can match. In addition, they use shorthand that most parents cannot decode on their own. The medium of texting, then, functionally divides parents from their children because the parents can only understand as much texting lingo as a nonnative speaker can understand of English.

Yet these kinds of cultural divisions don't have to lead to negative experiences. Children and parents can help each other adjust to cultural changes, and with patience they can understand one another. Older and younger pastors can work together to understand the whole of their congregations and how to communicate the gospel to them. However, this doesn't always happen, and the techno-cultural divide between parents and children—and the older and younger groups in a congregation—often becomes a major source of conflict.

These technologically driven cultural divides have also become much more common in the last century than at any other time in history. As we mentioned in chapter 4, changes in communication mediums happened very slowly before around 1850. The time between the dawn of Cain's civilization to the invention of writing was thousands of years. Then several more thousand years passed between the advent of writing and the invention of the printing press. But for the past century or so, new or updated communication mediums are invented every time we turn on the radio, turn on the TV, turn on the laptop, turn on the cell phone, or turn on the device invented after this book is published.

Each of these new tools comes with the ability to communicate different kinds of meaning and to create a new culture intimately familiar with its use. People in that new culture will see the world in a slightly different way, not only because they communicate through different mediums but because they think differently. This is because in addition to creating culture, mediums also shape the way we think.

Mediums Shape Thinking

My dear friend Trey is one of the most gifted photographers I know. In fact, I don't really think of him as someone who "takes pictures" but rather as someone who "creates images" that are clearly works of art.

I've been with him as he shoots, and sometimes I think there is no way he'll be able to capture anything worthwhile because there just isn't anything interesting there. But inevitably, he always returns with an image that is simply stunning. Over time, I've come to believe that he sees the world differently than I do. He has spent years training his eyes to see the world the way his camera does. This allows him to go to war-torn southern Sudan and capture the radiance of a child's face and the dignity of a pastor who has almost nothing. Trey has intentionally cultivated this skill and has dedicated himself to thinking like a camera. One might say he doesn't think *about* the camera, he thinks *through* the camera.

Whether we intend to or not, anytime we use a medium we, like Trey, are training our minds to think according to its patterns. While the camera literally changes the way we see the world, other mediums also present us with distinct ways of conceiving of the world. The more we use them, the more our minds adapt to their patterns. However, if we are using a technology natively—that is, if we were introduced to it from birth—it is difficult to detect these shifts in thinking patterns.

In the remainder of this chapter, we'll talk about two technologies—the printing press and photography—that have brought major shifts in the way we think about and see the world. Today's teenagers were born into the world of the Internet, but everyone born in the last five hundred years was born into a world of printed books. And every person born in the last 150 years was born into a world of photographs. Each of these changes in media brought with them a change in meaning, a change in culture, and a change in thinking patterns.

Printing Press. Discussions about the invention of the printing press in 1440 usually mention that a major cultural shift followed, bringing the Scientific Revolution, the Protestant Reformation, and democratic nations like the United States. We often say that this was because the lower cost of printed books allowed scientists to share information more quickly and gave individual Christians access to Bibles without needing to go through the Roman Catholic Church.

But the new level of access to information is only half the story. The printing press also brought with it a radical, new way of thinking embedded in the technology itself and the way we tend to use it. Two major features built into the technology of printed books are uniformity and complex linear thought.

Before the printing press, books were hand copied and each copy would look slightly different, with minor variations from copy to copy. But printed books are completely uniform. Every letter is rendered with precision, and every page of every copy of every book looks exactly the same. Due to lower costs, printed books can contain longer, more complex ideas than speech or the written word can readily handle.

The printed book, then, encourages things like uniformity, accuracy, and complex linear thoughts; and it turns out these are features of the Scientific Revolution as well as much of the theological work that followed it. Certainly, there was science before the printing press and theology before the Enlightenment, but the kind of science and theology we find after the printing press can be characterized as particularly bookish. For example, throughout church history, we find church leaders like Origen, Augustine, and Thomas Aquinas working to organize the theology found throughout the Scriptures in a systematic way. But those thinkers were also comfortable with finding allegorical and metaphorical meanings in the biblical stories. However, as more printed books became available, literacy began to spread, which gave way to an emphasis on "literal" interpretation. By the time of Luther and Calvin, allegorical interpretation was largely looked down upon, and in centuries that followed theology became more and more sciencelike until systematic theology became nearly the only way of doing theology.[4]

During Calvin's lifetime, another technology was invented that radically shaped the thinking of everyday Christians. That technology was the chapter and verse numbers that were added to the Scriptures. Before this time, the text of the Bible did not come with any consistent numbering system. Each book was simply one long block of text divided into paragraphs, much like this book. But during the 1550s when the print era was in full swing, scholars created the chapter and verse numbering system and began including it in published editions of the Bible.[5]

The new numbering system made it much easier for theologians to refer to passages of Scripture in a consistent manner. But by adding the chapter and verse numbers, they had in a sense effectively systematized the Scripture itself. Today, whenever we open a Bible, we see the Word of God through this layer of technology, and we interpret the Scriptures according to this technological way of thinking. When we talk about our favorite verses or hold up signs at sporting events (John 3:16), we are performing technologically enabled activities.

As we've said before, technology is the means by which we transform what God has made, and the technology of the printed Bible—with its versification system—fits that definition very well. Verse numbers literally reshape the text of Scripture and subsequently the thinking of the one who reads it. Verse numbers were created as a means to navigate Scriptures quickly; but because means and ends are always connected, the means of verse numbers has brought with it the end of thinking about the Bible as a book of verses. Of course, I don't mean to imply that chapter and verse numbers are morally wrong—on the contrary, they are extremely helpful, and I am grateful for them. However, we must recognize that the technology of verses has the power to influence as much as it helps.

The printed book, like all other technology, is value-laden. Printed books value things like objectivity, uniformity, structure, and logic. And when we look at the culture and thinkers who were native book readers, we find that way of thinking embedded in their thoughts and ideas.

Photography. Photography, which became more common beginning around 1850, implies a different set of values and a different kind of thinking. When we read a printed book, we often forget that we are spending a lot of our mental energy converting letters into words, and then forming those words into sentences, concepts, and ideas. This is a skill that we learn in school and perfect with years of practice. But when we look at a picture, no translation is necessary. We are born with all the tools we need to understand images.

We could spend an entire chapter detailing differences between print and images, but one of the key differences that media scholars often point to is that while printed text is particularly good at conveying linear, abstract data, images are much better at drawing us into a concrete story and evoking an emotional reaction. Shane Hipps, in his book *Flickering Pixels*, points out that the old adage, "A picture is worth a thousand words," isn't really accurate. "It would seem a picture is actually worth a thousand emotions."[6] He gives the example of the difference between our reactions to a printed sentence like "The boy is sad" and a picture of a starving child, crying in the middle of a scorched African plain. The printed sentence presents us with abstract concepts, but the picture immediately pulls on our hearts. When we see words, they cause us to think; but when we see a picture, we react first and then think about our reaction afterward.

The power that images have to draw us into a story and evoke an emotional response can be seen in two important areas of modern life. The first is the way advertisers use images to associate positive emotions with the product they sell. All an advertiser must do is connect something that elicits a strong emotional response (e.g., a cute baby, a beautiful woman, or an image of power) to a product, and our minds automatically associate the two.

Before photography was common, advertising mostly consisted of a list of features and specifications for a product. But today, advertisers focus less on features and more on feeling. Car commercials don't just tell you about their seating capacity, the commercial shows you happy, powerful, and sexy people sitting in those seats. And the commercial invites you to picture yourself in the driver's seat. Razor commercials don't just tell you that the product will give you a close, nick-free shave; they show you that such a shave will help you attract happy, powerful, and sexy people of the opposite gender. Every commercial for every product uses the power of images to link that product to emotions of happiness, power, and sex.

It is that last category—sex—that dominates advertising. God designed sexuality to be one of the most powerful physical and emotional forces a human can experience, and so it only makes sense that advertisers would tap into this power constantly. Sadly, the power of sensual images is also evident through the epidemic of pornography that is quickly spreading throughout the world. In pornography we find that what God had designed to be a private, unmediated union of a committed man and woman has been distorted into a publicly available but privately accessed illusion of connection that happens through a screen-mediated look at an unmediated (i.e., unclothed) human being.

It is said that pornographers have always been at the forefront of every communication technology. Pornography was one of the first things distributed on printed books, and it quickly found its way into the world of images. In recent years, the pornography industry was a major factor in the battle between VHS and Beta and Blu-ray over HD-DVD, and it will likely drive future home entertainment mediums like 3D television.

Christians who battle the sin of pornography are right to focus on the physical, sexual lust that the images evoke. However, one of the deeper and often overlooked reasons people become addicted to pornography is the power of the medium itself. Men and women become addicted not just to the physical response the images elicit, but even more dangerously, to the way the images powerfully affect the emotions and seem to offer temporary relief from the hurts, pressures, and pains of life. Getting out of pornography then is not only a matter of understanding that the content is sinful (not to mention exploitative), but also understanding how the medium of images works upon the mind, heart, and soul.[7]

Of course, this doesn't mean that images are always morally corrupt. But neither does it mean that images are a neutral medium where the only thing that matters is the content itself. No, as we've been saying, images as a medium shape our thinking and communicate meaning. Sometimes this meaning contains a powerful theological truth.

In the last chapter, we found that God restricted the use of carved images in Israelite worship. The early church debated whether or not this commandment should still apply in the New Testament era. More specifically, they wondered if it was permissible to make images that represented Jesus. For several centuries, they debated this issue (now called the Iconoclast Controversy), holding several councils that went back and forth on the use of "icons"[8] in worship. In the end, a final council concluded that icons of Jesus could in fact be used in Christian worship. Their reasoning was that the act of making an image of Jesus is a kind of replaying of the incarnation. To them, images of Jesus were a theological reinforcement of the fact that the Son of God took on human form. The great theologian of that era, John of Damascus, wrote:

> When the Invisible One becomes visible to flesh then you may then draw a likeness of His form. When He who is a pure spirit, without form or limit, immeasurable in the boundlessness of His own nature, existing as God, takes upon Himself the form of a servant in substance and in stature, and a body of flesh, then you may draw His likeness, and show it to anyone willing to contemplate it.[9]

Some Christians today still feel it is impermissible to make images of Jesus, yet the entire debate is itself based on the wonder of the incarnation. Even a profane image of Jesus recalls the truth that God came to dwell among his people.

So what kind of thinking patterns, cultural changes, and meanings do digital mediums like radio, television, and the Internet bring with them? Books and books have been written attempting to explore these changes, and we attempt to surface some of these issues in chapter 11. But before we get to the age of the Internet, we need to finish telling the biblical story and see what role, if any, technology has in the new heavens and new earth that God has promised.

9

RESTORATION

I haven't kept up with soccer since I used to play it as a kid, but as I was writing this book, something in the 2010 World Cup caught my eye. I saw reports that players were complaining about the new high-tech ball that Adidas had introduced that year called the Jabulani.

I did some research on soccer balls and found that this wasn't the first time players had complained about a new kind of ball. During the 2002 World Cup, Adidas introduced the new Fevernova ball, featuring a new syntactic foam layer and a three-layer knitted chassis designed to make the ball follow a more consistent and predicable flight pattern than the previous generation of balls. However, while the Fevernova accomplished this goal, many players complained that it was too light, making it fly unpredictably. The Fevernova also had the age-old problem of taking on water during raining matches, which degraded its performance.

So for the 2006 World Cup, Adidas attempted to fix those problems with their new +Teamgeist ball. Instead of the traditional thirty-two hexagons and pentagons found in most balls, the new +Teamgeist had fourteen curved panels that were bonded together rather than stitched. This goal was to make the ball uniformly round and completely waterproof. Yet for all of Adidas's efforts in solving the water problem, some players felt that the ball flew too fast. It was too easy to score goals they said, and it made goalies look slow and ineffective.

Adidas again made further improvements for the 2010 World Cup ball called the Jabulani. They further reduced the number of panels from fourteen down to eight, but they also added textured grooves to the panels intended to make the ball have the same kind of aerodynamics as a traditional stitched ball. But as with the previous iterations, some players complained that the new grooves made the ball fly unpredictably. Undoubtedly someone at Adidas is now working furiously on the 2014 ball, attempting to add new features while avoiding the problems of the previous generation.

The recent history of the soccer ball has exposed something we don't always like to admit—that every good technology comes with a trade-off of some kind. Newer tools bring us benefits, but those benefits come with a cost. Even the VP of Product at Facebook, Chris Cox, admitted as much when he said, "Facebook solved this problem of getting all your friends in one place, and created the problem of having all your friends in one place."[1] Mobile phones allow us to call for help from almost anywhere, but they also allow everyone else to reach us no matter where we go. It would be almost irresponsible *not* to carry a phone on a hiking trip and yet the presence of the phone changes the experience of the natural world.

Even when inventors have the best of intentions for their creations, there are always some people who get swept up in the ever-changing torrent of technological change. As Neil Postman said, "the advantages and disadvantages of new technologies are never distributed evenly among the population. This means that every new technology benefits some and harms others." Horseshoe makers lose out to automobile manufacturers, and local coffee shops get driven out by massive corporations. Robotic factories make products cheaper for some, but those same robots push others out of a job. We could spend chapter after chapter outlining these trade-offs and still not uncover all the new problems that technology can bring.

For some, this talk of trade-offs and imbalances stirs up fears that technology is destroying human life as we know it. Some wonder if one day all this technology will implode upon us bringing an end to civilization as we know it. Sci-fi writers spend much of their time exploring what life would look like after a technological apocalypse sends us to a futuristic dark age. Yet these worries typically leave out an important detail—the way the biblical story ends, and the role technology plays in that ending.

As believers, it is in the incarnation, death, resurrection, and return of Jesus that we find our hope and our salvation. In this final stage of the biblical story—restoration—we also find answers to some of our remaining questions regarding technology. As we'll soon see, Jesus himself was a creator and user of technology, using tools to transform the natural world for practical purposes. But even more importantly, Jesus' interaction with certain human creations—the cross and the city—serve as a metaphor for understanding the powerful transformation that he is in the process of completing. After we've looked at this promised restoration, we will assemble what we've learned into something we can use to examine any technology.

Jesus, the Technologist and Transformer

In the Greek New Testament, Jesus and his father's job title is the Greek word *tektōn*, which is related to our English term "technology." As we saw in chapter 4, *tektōn* meant "artisan" or "skilled worker" in Jesus' day, and tradition has long held that the kind of skilled work that Jesus and Joseph did was carpentry.

According to our definition, Jesus and his father would have been "doing technology" when they used tools to transform pieces of wood into something useful. It is interesting to see that Jesus' day job fits well within the call to "cultivate and keep the garden" from Genesis, but his carpentry also functions as a validation of his human nature and redemptive work.

When the Greek *tektōn* is translated to Latin, it becomes *faber;* and, as we mentioned before, some anthropologists believe that *homo faber* ("skilled man" or "making man") is the best way to describe humans because our

creation of and dependence upon tools is what sets us apart evolution-
arily from other animals. Ironically, then, by the standard of nonbelieving
anthropologists, the kind of work that Jesus did could not be more fundamentally human. Although Jesus would later be known by the title of
"Rabbi," the title *tektōn* powerfully affirms the fullness of his human nature.
And in a wonderful twist, God the Father orchestrated the story so that the
day job of his Son would encompass the very thing—technology—that we
sometimes mistake for hope.

Of course, the significance of Jesus' work on earth was not carpentry but
what he did on the cross. And yet technology had a part to play there as
well. In another strange irony, the technology with which Jesus worked—
wood and nails—was the technology on which he died—a cross.

Jesus could have been executed using any number of more "natural"
means, but in God's great plan the way he died was decidedly technological.
Under Jewish law he could have been stoned (cf. John 8:59)—which would
have employed naturally occurring rocks rather than a carefully constructed
cross. Likewise, he could have been drowned, poisoned, strangled, thrown
from a cliff (cf. Luke 4:29), or handed over to lions, any of which would
have been less tool-oriented than crucifixion, one of "making man's" most
horrific creations.

The gospel of John begins by telling us that the entire world and everything
in it was created by the Son of God. God had again become immediate, walking among his creations. But then John tells us that Jesus "came unto his own
but his own did not receive him." In other words, the Creator was rejected
by his own creation. This rejection reached its culmination in the cross when
God's highest creation used the creative powers he gave them to create a tool
designed to put their Creator to death. In the cross, we find the Son of God
rejected by the humans he created with his heavenly Father, and the Son of
Man murdered by the tools he and his earthly father used. At Golgotha, Jesus
hung naked and bloody from a tree that he had spoken into existence, but that
humans had transformed into a tool of death. The cross, then, is a symbol of
the distorted creation turning on its creator. That twisted tree represents the
twisted us, a humanity transformed by sin and bent toward death.

Why, then, do we wear these grotesque distortions of sin around our necks? Why are they on top of our churches and in the background of our PowerPoint slides?

It is because Christ's transformative power goes beyond wood and nails. He has declared that the cross is no longer a symbol of deformation but of the transformative work Christ accomplished for us. Whenever we attempt to transform the natural world for destructive purposes, the cross says that God can transform that evil and restore what was lost.

After he died, Joseph of Arimathea placed Jesus' body in a tomb that someone had carved out of the ground. In addition to serving as the practical place to put a dead body, tombs function as a cultural symbol of the finality of death. Yet when the resurrected Jesus emerged from the tomb having triumphed over sin and death, he transformed the tomb into a symbol that now serves the opposite for which it was intended.[2] In his death and resurrection, Jesus transformed the cross and the grave from symbols of death to symbols of life and the transformation that his Spirit begins to work when we believe that he is the Christ, the Son of God.

When we move out of the Gospels into the book of Revelation, we find that God has promised to continue transforming human creations meant for evil into things meant for good.

A New City for a New Earth

Back in Genesis 4, Cain built the first city in his attempt to establish an anti-garden, a place where he could distract himself from his fallenness and live apart from God. Throughout the remainder of the Scriptures, whenever "the city" is mentioned it is always in the context of curses and evil. Yet when God created the nation of Israel, he began to hint that he would not only restore humanity; he would also restore many of the creations of humanity, including the city.

This begins with God commanding the Israelites to designate six of their cities as places of refuge for foreigners (Num. 36:15). God was asking his people to use cities in a way that was contrary to their built-in tendencies of use. Instead of using them to keep foreigners out, the Israelites were to use them to invite people in.

God also chose the city of Jerusalem as the place where he would dwell with his people, first in the tabernacle and later in the temple of Solomon. But even the presence of God in Zion could not make a people broken and twisted by sin follow the Law and live holy lives. Even God's handcrafted cultural goods and practices in his chosen city could not save his people. From Solomon onward, the Israelite kings worshipped idols; and the Old Testament prophets repeatedly tell of God's wrath against their sin and the sin of the people. Here is Micah's judgment against them: "Therefore because of you Zion shall be plowed as a field; Jerusalem shall become a heap of ruins, and the mountain of the house a wooded height" (Mic. 3:12).

And yet in his grace, God has still chosen the most fallen and rebellious of human creations as the place for his final restoration. God made a promise to the people of Jerusalem to restore their city, not because it was a good or worthy city, but as a symbol of God's redemptive work in which he transforms unworthy things into holy things. The very next verse in Micah portrays the restoration of Jerusalem with God again dwelling among his creations as he did in the garden. Micah says that the "the peoples" will flow into the "the house of the LORD" upon Zion so that "he may teach us his ways and that we might walk in his paths" (Mic. 4:1–2). Micah's vision of the future also involves people transforming their technologies of destruction into those of cultivation: "they shall beat their swords into plowshares, and their spears into pruning hooks; nation shall not lift up sword against nation, neither shall they learn war anymore" (Mic. 4:3; cf. Isa. 2:4). The Old Testament visions of the future are focused on the removal of sin and the dwelling of God among his people, and the place of this restoration is always the city.

Then at the end of the biblical story, when God takes the final step in his plan of redemption by restoring all things, the restoration of the city reaches its culmination. When John's Revelation tells of God creating the new heavens and new earth for the resurrected and redeemed human race (Rev. 21:1), it makes no mention of God re-creating the Garden of Eden. Instead of a garden, John tells us that God will bring down from heaven a redeemed and restored city. John spends nearly the entire chapter describing all the natural materials God will use for this transformation, as he fills his city with human creations like buildings, roads, and trumpets. Ellul concludes his study of the city in the Scriptures with these words: "Thus the history of the city, divided in two by Jesus Christ, goes from Eden to Jerusalem, from a garden to a city."[3]

This promise of this new city tells us that God's plan is not merely to regenerate human bodies and resurrect human souls but also to restore human creations to a world untainted by sin. Our souls are stained with sin, our bodies are destined for death, and our creations cause as many problems as they solve, but God has promised to restore them all. In the new city there will be no more sadness, pain, or death, only everlasting joy and glory to God. And although the Bible doesn't make this explicit, we can only assume that some human creations—including tools—will also be restored such that they too are free from the trade-offs and unintended consequences that cripple them today.

When God removes from us the ability to sin, we will no longer use technology for rebellion against him. But we can also be hopeful that God will remove the problems we cause with our tools as well. What this looks like is beyond our imagination or speculation. Revelation even hints that some technology, like artificial light, will be rendered obsolete merely by the presence of the Son of God in our midst:

> And the city has no need of sun or moon to shine on it, for
> the glory of God gives it light, and its lamp is the Lamb.
> (Rev. 21:23)

The presence of Emmanuel, whose name means "God With Us," among his people is our greatest hope. The nonmediated God, physically present with us, will be our greatest joy.

And yet in his city there appears a small but important place for our tools. In fact, after Jesus rose from the dead, he gave us an enduring portrait of how we might use tools in a restored earth.

The Day God Made Breakfast

In the epilogue of his gospel, John tells of an encounter between the resurrected Jesus and his apostles. Jesus had already appeared to Mary and the disciples twice, revealing that he had been resurrected from the dead and encouraging them to continue in faith.

Then in John 21, we find the story of Peter's restoration. After Jesus repeated his miracle of helping the disciples catch a boatload of fish, John writes, "When they got out on land, they saw a charcoal fire in place, with fish laid out on it, and bread" (John 21:9). (It is rather striking that Jesus, in his resurrected and glorified body, would take the time to prepare a fire and make breakfast for the disciples!)

In preparing this breakfast, Jesus used simple tools to create a space for an embodied encounter between himself and Peter, and then he used that space to restore Peter to his appointed place as the leader of the disciples. Remember that the last time John told us about "a charcoal fire" was in John 18:18, when Peter denied Jesus before the men warming themselves by the fire in the high priest's courtyard. Therefore, the fire in our current breakfast scene takes on new significance for Peter (and the gospel reader), as Jesus transforms the meaning of fire from the place where Peter sinned to the place where Peter was restored.

Notice that the glorified Jesus didn't use an awe-inspiring miracle like a burning bush to approach Peter; rather, he simply used the tools of the day—charcoal—to make a meal of fish and bread. Again, we see Jesus playing the role of a transformer, taking the tool of Peter's rebellion and transforming it into a tool for restoration.

We who live in the period between the garden and the city should notice that the Son of God was using tools even after his resurrection. He didn't attempt to use tools to solve deep spiritual problems but rather to enable a deep, full, complete human connection. John tells us that Jesus "became flesh and dwelt among us" (John 1:14), and the word for "dwelt" can also be translated "tabernacled," which involves an act of making. The Son of God "tabernacled" among us in order to do his work of salvation, and here with Peter he is again performing an act of "making" by creating a place for physical presence and spiritual restoration. After John tells of the city coming down from heaven, he says, "And I heard a loud voice from the throne, saying, 'Behold, the *tabernacle* of God is among men, and He will dwell among them, and they shall be His people, and God Himself will be among them'" (Rev. 21:3 NASB).

Until that day, the New Testament urges us to use physical tools—specifically the Table and the Cup—to create a space for the embodied fellowship of believers. Throughout the Epistles, Paul, Peter, and John express their deep desire to be physically present with those to whom they wrote.[4] Often, the apostle writers connect "joy" and "fullness" to being physically present, and they report sadness and longing when they must resort to communication tools like writing. And yet, as we see in John's epistles (2 John 12; 3 John 12–13), they still used communication tools when embodied encounters were not possible and when the use of those tools could build up the body of Christ. However, their intention was to honor the incarnation of Christ by always holding physical presence as the highest and best medium.

These two eschatological images from John—of our resurrected Lord cooking breakfast and the glorified Lord bringing down a restored city—tell us that our hope resides in the presence of God among his people. But they also tell us that we shouldn't view technology as a temporary aberration of the fallen world. Instead, Jesus has offered a portrait of technology according to God's original design, for his glory, and for the building up of the body of Christ through embodied life. Our tools are still flawed and problematic, but we have the promise that God will somehow restore even them to a sinless state. This final aspect of technology will allow us to create a tool through which we can evaluate all of our technology today.

A Tetrad of Technology

As we've looked at the biblical story, we've divided it into four acts: Creation, Fall, Redemption, and Restoration, and relabeled them Reflection, Rebellion, Redemption, and Restoration. In each of these chapters, we've observed the role technology played in the story of God and his people, and then asked philosophically oriented questions about the meaning of tools. We can now assemble what we've learned into a framework for examining technology.

First, from the story of creation, we found that our ability to make technology is a *reflection* of our Creator. Among the things we create, technology is the "human activity of using tools to transform God's creation for practical purposes." Our mobile phones, for example, reflect God's nature as relational and communicative, and they transform the physical space of the world.

Second, from the fall, we found that every technology has the potential to be used for sin and *rebellion*. Though a mobile phone is not itself morally evil, it cannot be considered "neutral" either. Instead, embedded in its design is a tendency of usage from which a set of values emerge. Our flesh will often seize upon the power and value system of a tool and use it for evil. People have found all kinds of ways to employ mobile phones in service of selfish gain and destruction.

But even though tools can be used for rebellion, we found that technology can be used for *redemptive* purposes, temporarily overcoming the effects of the fall and serving the embodied life of Christ in the believer. Mobile phones can connect those who cannot be physically present, and they can be used to coordinate meeting times and places. However, we also found that mediums are powerful shapers of culture and thinking. Moreover, for all the good that mobile phones offer, they also bring with them a series of trade-offs and unintended consequences.

Thankfully, at the end of the biblical story, we find that God's plans include the *restoration* of all things, including some of the things we make. Normally we think of *restoration* in purely positive terms, but here we'll use the category of *restoration* to highlight the problems technology can cause that are in need of restoration. If possible, we should work toward restoring them ourselves, but some problems will never be relieved until the new city arrives.

We can now put these four parts of the biblical story in a simple chart form:

| 1. Reflection | 4. Restoration |
| 3. Redemption | 2. Rebellion |

At first glance, the four chapters might look out of order, but don't be alarmed—I've arranged them this way in order to surface additional relationships between them. The two down the left column—Reflection and Redemption—highlight the positive things that can happen with technology, while the two down the right column—Rebellion and Restoration—bring out negative aspects of technology. The rows are also aligned to show that the top two boxes—Reflection and Restoration—are both unintentional aspects of technology while the bottom row—Redemption and Rebellion—are things we do intentionally.

This allows us to augment our chart with the following categories:

	Positive	Negative
Unintentional	1. Reflection	4. Restoration
Intentional	3. Redemption	2. Rebellion

We've already mentioned some of the intentionally positive (redemptive) and intentionally negative (rebellious) uses of mobile phones, but to truly understand how the tool functions, we need to spend more time on the unintentional categories (the top row of the chart).

For example, even when a phone "maker" isn't intentionally trying to honor God with his creation, what he makes is still a reflection of his Creator. Steve Jobs, Michael Dell, and Bill Gates don't claim to be Christians, but their products reflect the creativity of God as well as the longings of the human heart. Their tools also bring with them certain trade-offs and unintended consequences, and for all the benefits they offer, sometimes we lose as much as we gain. We remain hopeful that God will eliminate these problems in the new city, but we cannot afford to ignore them today.

The category of *restoration* is not meant to be an excuse in regard to the problems of technology. On the contrary, carefully considering the trade-offs and problems of technology should urge us to create and use tools that fit within God's command to both "cultivate" and "keep" the garden. And if we are not in the position of creating such tools, we need to spend time thinking about the value systems that emerge from using a tool; we must discern when those tools are in conflict with the value system of the kingdom of God. Just as the promise of resurrection does not imply that we are free to neglect our souls and bodies, the promise to restore our tools does not give us license to create or use tools that abuse God's creation and distort the kind of life he has commanded us to live.

Thinking about technology through this tetrad of questions also gives us an opportunity to worship God whenever we use tools. When something works well, it is reflecting the order and creativity of God. Rather than praising Apple, we can praise the God who created Steve Jobs in his image. When something enables us to further God's kingdom and restore something that was lost in the fall, we again have the chance to praise God for graciously allowing us to create even in our sinful state. But we must also be ardent in our insistence that the redemptive capacities of technology are limited and temporary. We cannot mistake their power for the power of the one who one day will finally redeem us. Instead, let us view the redemptive functions of our tools as a foreshadowing of what is to come.

At the same time when we see unspeakable evil conducted with and through technology, it is not cause for us to hate or fear technology but for us to hate the sin that shackles us all. And when we run into technology failures and problems—dropped calls, the Blue Screen of Death, smog, and so on— let's not curse our tools like fools do. Instead, when the medicine no longer works, let us redirect our hope away from our tools and to the one who will restore all human things, human souls, human bodies, and human creations.

In the next two chapters, we will pick up the history of technology where the Bible leaves off and explore two major technological periods, both of which seek to overrule and deny the way the Bible looks at technology. First, we'll talk about the advances in mechanical tools that took place from the 1500s to the 1800s that helped reinforce Cain's idea that humans can live happily apart from God. Then in chapter 11, we'll finally reach the electronic era in which we now live and attempt to surface the kind of culture and values it engenders.

TECHNICISM

It's not uncommon for technology magazines and blogs to display the words, "The future is going to be awesome!" They tell us of fantastic devices that will make things easier, faster, and better and will solve all of our problems. Sometimes we even find the makers and purveyors of technology promising that a new tool such as the "One Laptop Per Child" initiative[1] will bring peace to war-torn regions of the world.

Yet when we look back into the history books of technological problems, we find that technological initiatives haven't always panned out. Kevin Kelly, in his book *What Technology Wants*, lists several tools whose creators promised that their devices would bring world peace.[2] For example, Hiram Maxim, the inventor of the machine gun, insisted his invention would "make war impossible." Alfred Nobel believed his invention, dynamite, would "sooner lead to peace than a thousand world conventions." When Nobel realized that his tool was bringing about the exact opposite, he founded the Nobel Prize in hopes that his legacy would be one of peace instead of destruction. But it wasn't just weapon makers who thought their tools could prevent war; Orville Wright believed that the airplane he and his brother invented would "have a tendency to make war impossible." Guglielmo Marconi believed his radio and "the coming wireless era" would "make war impossible." The promises of technologically enabled peace go on and on.

In a sense, this promise goes all the way back to humanity's first days outside the Garden of Eden. While the people of God place their hope in God's promise to restore his creation, wipe away our sins, resurrect our bodies, and bring down a glorious new city from heaven, the enemies of God tell an alternate story. Beginning with Cain, the alternative vision says that humans will find their salvation in the city and its technology. The city presents us a welcome distraction from our sin, and its power creates the illusion that we can live apart from God. One day, we tell ourselves, the technology of the city will become our savior, rescuing us even from death. As St. Augustine wrote long ago,

> [The] two cities have been formed out of two loves: the earthly [city] by the love of the self, even to the contempt of God; the heavenly [city] by the love of God, even to the contempt of self. The former, in a word, glories in itself, the latter in the Lord. For the one seeks glory from men; but the greatest glory of the other is God.[3]

Today we can see these two divergent views of technology in the way our culture conceives of "progress." As modern people, we tend to believe that technology is always progressing, and that any problems caused by technology can be solved by applying more technology to the technological problems. Of course technology often does solve problems, and later generations of technology tend to have fewer problems than the first generation. However, over time our culture has begun to believe that technology will one day solve *all* of our problems, leading to a kind of utopia. Stephen Monsma calls this idea "technicism,"[4] and he argues that it has become a kind of unspoken religion for the secular world. For those who don't see

God as an anchoring point for reality, technological progress has become a means of salvation and a source of future hope.

In this and the following chapter, we will follow the thread of Cain's city as the anti-garden and see how this theme weaved its way through human history after the close of the biblical canon. We will begin by looking at a major turning point in history, from what philosophers call "premodernity" to "modernity" taking place around 1650 and coinciding with the rise of physically oriented machine technology. In the next chapter, we'll come to the present digital world where the city is no longer constructed from flesh and blood but from bits and bytes.

The Rise of the Machines

In the centuries between about 1200 and 1600, there was a flurry of intellectual, scientific, and technological development throughout Europe. During the Renaissance, major works of art such as Michelangelo's Sistine Chapel and sculpture of David were created. Then in the Scientific Revolution, thinkers like Copernicus, Kepler, Newton, and even Galileo made major discoveries about the laws of physics and how the universe works. At the same time, men like Leonardo da Vinci began experimenting with ever more complex and powerful tools, drawing up plans for everything from helicopters to firearms. Accurate timekeeping tools were also invented during this period, as well as ships with ranges long enough to explore the "New World."

Over time, as these developments stacked up, people began to think of these new tools in terms of "mastery over nature." For the first time philosophers started to speak of progress not in moral or civil terms but in relationship to advances in technology. As technology progressed, it gave humanity more and more control over the natural world, and people began to hope it would one day remove all human suffering from the planet. Many of these thinkers were Christians such as Francis Bacon who wrote,

> For man by the fall fell at the same time from his state of
> innocence and from his dominion over creation. Both of

these losses, however, can even in this life be in some part repaired; the former by religion and faith, the latter by arts and sciences.[5]

But notice that Bacon sees two separate problems with two separate solutions. The first problem is the stain of sin that Bacon believes that God alone can repair. But as for the second problem, dominion over creation, Bacon thinks that technology (i.e., "arts and sciences") can do some good. However, he is guarded in his hope about technology, saying it can only solve problems "in some part." But over time, many thinkers rejected this limited expectation of technology and began to see science and technology as a means of freeing humanity from their need for God, from sin, and even from mortality.

Somewhere around 1650, in the middle of this scientific and technological progress, historians see a major shift in the way people conceived of the world. The period before 1650 is often called the "premodern" period, and after 1650 is referred to as the "modern" period. In the premodern period, almost everyone was religious in the sense of believing in a God or gods who set in place the fixed moral rules of the world. In fact, just about everything in life was fixed: where people lived, their jobs, the location of the nearby river or distant mountain—all of these were fixed points, just like the laws of the universe given by the gods.

But the technological advances in the centuries leading up to the 1600s meant that people no longer had to see the world as a set of fixed objects. Rivers could now be redirected, and mountains could now be moved. But moving mountains no longer required faith the size of a mustard seed, only sufficiently advanced technology and science.

The philosophers of the day started to write that if the objects in the world were not fixed, then maybe the moral and religious laws of the universe weren't either. And if there are no fixed moral laws, then there is no problem of innocence to overcome. The generations after Bacon argued that "spiritual" problems were the creation of imaginary religions, but science tells us that our problems are only physical and that technology can eventually overcome them all.

At the time, most Europeans were Christians who believed that one day Christ would return to make all things right. When they looked at a time-line of history, they saw the return of Christ at the end. But in the shift from "premodernity" to "modernity," Jesus was kicked off the end of the timeline and replaced with technology. In previous eras, atheism had never been a truly viable belief system, and it attracted few people. But as science and technology continued to progress, the need for God appeared to grow dimmer and dimmer. The power of technology was one of the factors that led Friedrich Nietzsche to make his famous declaration that "God is dead." Of course, Nietzsche didn't mean that God had literally died—he meant that the story we've been telling ourselves about a God who runs the uni-verse no longer made any sense in a world where humans could control the natural world with technology. Nietzsche believed that humanity needed a new story to replace the one about God. It turns out that technology offered the perfect replacement.

In fact, technicism has all the elements of a good religion. It has a savior, which in this case, is obviously technology. It has prophets and preachers— the commercials that continually remind us of the greatness of the lords and saviors. Technicism also has a future hope (or eschatology) called the "sin-gularity," which is when our computers become smarter than all of human-ity put together, and they gain the ability to invent tools that our tiny little minds can't even imagine. Technicism even has a concept of salvation and eternal life, which will occur when the post-singularity computers invent tools that enable all humans to live forever, ushering in the post-human era.

Post-humanism (sometimes called trans-humanism) is the belief that with enough technological enhancements humans will eventually evolve beyond our current limitations, enabling us to become powerful beings who live forever. Futurist Ray Kurzweil writes, "I regard the freeing of the human mind from its severe physical limitations of scope and duration as the necessary next step in evolution. Evolution, in my view, represents the purpose of life. That is, the purpose of life—and of our lives—is to evolve."[6] Kurzweil goes on to write that the advancement of technology is a kind of spiritual ascension where humankind is moving ever upward, eventually leading to a place where we free ourselves from the physical world and live in a heavenlike state.

Now, most people don't go as far as Kurzweil in openly confessing with their mouths that technology is lord and savior. If you ask the average person if technology is the "savior of humanity," you probably won't get an acknowledgment of that kind of language.[7] And yet these characteristics of technicism—an overconfidence about technology and a devaluing of physical, embodied life—have found their way into many aspects of our modern world. In the centuries that ensued, additional technological developments have worked, quite literally, to drive the message home.

I'm Not a Luddite, But . . .

The valuing of technology over human life reached its apex in what is now known as the Luddite controversy. During the Industrial Revolution, many of the new machines that were invented were designed to perform tasks more efficiently than individual workers. This new manufacturing equipment allowed business owners to increase their profits because they could replace ten laborers with a single person who pushed a button on a machine. The problem was that the other nine men lost their jobs.

With no way to earn money for their families, many fell into poverty and despair. According to legend, in 1779 a man named Ned Ludd was fed up with the takeover of the machines and took his anger out on two knitting machines. The news of Ned's rage against the machines spread quickly, and groups of masked men fed up with their livelihood being taken over by machines started breaking into factories all over England and destroying manufacturing equipment. Whenever a machine was found destroyed, people would whisper, "Ned Ludd did it."

It's easy to see how the term "Luddite" became associated with the fear of technology and technological change. But the writings the Luddites left behind indicate that their main concern was not technology itself, but the fact that technological thinking had convinced business owners to value their machines more than human life. In fact, in 1721, the British government made machine destruction a capital offense. God had said, "Whoever sheds the blood of man, by man shall his blood be shed, for God made man in his own image" (Gen. 9:6). But the new laws said in effect, "Whoever sheds the blood of a machine, by a machine shall his blood be shed, for man has made machines his god."

While many of the Luddites were simply angry that they lost their jobs and livelihoods—and their acts of destruction were clearly wrong—it is hard to disagree with their sentiment that humankind had made the turn toward valuing machine life more than human life. And while very few people would ascribe to that view today, more subtle forms of this antihuman, protechnology spirit were found in the rise of consumerist capitalism and advertising that came on the heels of the Industrial Revolution.

Tell Me What I Need

The technological advances of the past few centuries—which we just described as leading to technicism—are as we've said not themselves morally evil. In fact, those advances brought humanity unprecedented material wealth and prosperity. Developments in medicine, plumbing, food preparation, and so on led to a world where average Europeans and Americans had access to clean water, adequate food, and sufficient shelter. The Industrial Revolution is known for many of its negative practices like child labor and filling the air with smog, but these new factories were able to efficiently produce basic goods at a low enough cost that even people with very little income could afford them. The standard of living in the industrialized world continued to grow steadily in decades leading up to 1900, leading to increased life expectancy and decreased infant mortality.

Then, around the turn of the twentieth century, things started to shift in an unforeseen direction. The factories were becoming so efficient at producing goods that they began making more goods than people previously needed. Today, the idea that a factory might produce something no one wants to buy is rather ordinary, but in the history of humanity this had never happened before. Basic goods were always scarce, as they still are today in developing countries, but suddenly factory owners were facing a question no one had ever asked before: "What do we do with all this extra stuff?"[8]

They had two choices before them. On one hand, they could choose to produce fewer goods. The problem with that approach is that it would mean running their machines less frequently and leaving excess capacity. It would mean higher costs of production and, therefore, higher prices. If prices went up, then competitors who chose not to decrease production could easily outsell them at lower prices. Ironically, the advances in manufacturing technology increased to a tipping point that threatened to destroy the prosperity it had created.

The second option for business owners was to keep producing as efficiently as possible, and then work to convince customers to buy things they didn't think they needed. This meant they needed to be more aggressive in telling potential customers about the benefits of their products. Up to that point, advertisements for products mostly consisted of the name, the price, and a list of the product's features. But soon a new technology would be perfected that could move customers in a way printed text never could: the photograph.

Advertisements soon started including not just a feature list but an image of the product. However, this wasn't enough to convince people to buy things they didn't think they needed. Eventually advertisers figured out that if they linked their products not just to a list of features, but to emotional feelings and even transcendent ideals, people would feel more compelled to buy them. For example, all one needs to get clean enough to be safe from germs is a simple bar of soap that costs almost nothing. But most of us don't buy the cheapest soap because we've been convinced that more expensive soaps will go beyond making us clean—they will make us feel happy.

It's that "feel happy" part that advertisers had to tap into to urge people to buy things that go above basic necessities. Advertisers created characters like the famous Marlboro man—a strong, loner cowboy—and men were convinced they could experience his life when they bought a pack of Marlboros. Today the company that has mastered the art of linking emotional images and transcendent wording to its products is Apple. Apple describes its products as "magical," "revolutionary," and "amazing." The original logo went so far as to put a happy rainbow on the symbol of sin and decay, the forbidden fruit. Today, that logo has been transformed into a brilliant, flawless white light reassuring us of its power and beauty.[9]

For advertisers, mastering language and images was only part of the problem. Two more issues were outstanding. First, advertisers needed a way to get those messages into homes. Newspapers and magazines weren't quite enough to deliver the sales volume they needed. They needed something more powerful and more pervasive. In the late 1800s, that powerful tool was created: the radio.

Radio technology was used quite effectively by the Allied and German militaries during World War I, but initially radio was too costly to have any use in the consumer market. Unlike newspapers, there was no way to charge listeners for the radio programs and therefore no way to make money from broadcasting. Yet advertisers knew that using radio to transmit commercials into homes would give them unprecedented public mind share, if only they could figure out a way to offer something other than twenty-four hour advertisements. So advertisers teamed up with people who wanted to broadcast news and stories, and together they found the right mix of advertising dollars and programming to make it all profitable.

In a way, the shows that people listened to—and later watched on television—were Trojan horses for advertisements. People loved listening to breaking news and hearing exciting stories, all paid for by advertisers whose goal was to inject into homes the message that new products and technology had the power to make their lives better. And they were terribly effective at getting this message across . . . leading to the next problem for advertisers.

Eventually, people started to believe that they needed all those excess goods the factories were pumping out. The problem was that people simply couldn't afford to buy them. Fortunately for product makers, there was an easy fix that would actually make them even more money. All they had to do was loan people the money they didn't have and convince them to pay it out over time—with interest.

The burgeoning credit market opened up more money to buy more things. Product makers continued to create new products, convincing people that buying them would bring happiness. Then they offered people more money to buy all of it. This powerful cycle continues today and, as we all know, it has started to catch up with us. The recent economic crisis that began in late 2008 can be traced back to that powerful moment when people were convinced that technology can make life better and—with just a little more credit—better life can be theirs right now.

Better Becomes a Moving Target

This is not to say that technology doesn't make anything better, for it certainly does that in many cases. We have access to unprecedented levels of prosperity, and we live in a world where almost anything is available at the push of a button. Only the most powerful kings of old could afford to taste the kinds of food anyone can buy at Walmart today, and only the most adventurous of history's sailors would ever set foot in the far-off lands that anyone with a valid passport can visit today. All accounts indicate that today's workers are in fact more productive on the whole than workers in previous generations. The US Bureau of Labor and Statistics, which has been tracking productivity since the 1960s, says that workers today are producing almost three times as much as workers fifty years ago.[10]

Yet this prosperity and productivity brings with it a shift in how we see the world and what we expect from it. To support all of this productivity and advancement, people began moving from the country into cities of ever-increasing size, and then into larger and larger homes in those cities. Families who once worked together on a farm now spent much of their day separated as Dad went off to work and Mom stayed home to care for the house. Thankfully, in the 1940s and 1950s many modern conveniences— vacuum cleaners, dishwashers, microwaves, and lawn mowers—came on the market, and many people believed these new devices would make work completely obsolete. They wondered if everyone would retire in their late thirties and sit around with nothing to do.

But this promise never materialized. Instead, people began to work more hours and have less free time. In her book, *More Work for Mother*,[11] Ruth Schartz Cowen argues that mothers actually took on *more* work during the "industrialization of the home" than ever before. How did this happen? Of course there were a variety of factors at play, but one of the major factors was the shifting of expectations. Before vacuum cleaners, people had to use brooms to clean their houses. Vacuum cleaners made housecleaning go much faster, but other changes counteracted this benefit. First, people started buying larger homes, giving them more to clean. Second, since fathers went to work in the city and families no longer lived near their friends, mothers were left with a larger workload to do in isolation. Finally, with all the new cleaning products and knowledge of germs and medicine, expectations of cleanliness shifted. The result was more to clean, more often, and with stronger tools. Instead of freeing up time to be with family and friends, there grew an expectation of what a person should have and how it should look. These shifts in expectations continue with every new technology.

In my pocket is a cell phone that is hundreds of times more powerful than the computer I had as a kid. Yet, I regularly think of things I wish it would do better, even though it does things I never imagined a phone could do just a few years ago. Each year a new soccer ball—like the World Cup balls we discussed in the previous chapter—comes along, solving some problems and introducing new ones. Of course, the new ball is usually better, but our definition of "better" has shifted as well. This cycle of progressive improvement and altered expectations has led to what we now call consumerism and materialism. Nothing is ever good enough, and we find ourselves continually distracted from our deeper spiritual needs that no tool can solve.

But even those of us who strive to put our treasure in the things of heaven are subject to one more subtle influence of modern technology. Not only do modern tools help reinforce technicism and perpetuate consumerism, the instant availability of today's technologies brings with it a fundamental change to human life, which most of us never even notice.

The Device Paradigm

Many people have pointed out that modern life goes so fast that almost everyone feels like they are behind. Even with our vacuum cleaners, dishwashers, and robotic lawn mowers, we can't keep up with everything that we want to do. We rush about from thing to thing and task to task, but at the end of the day, we don't always feel fulfilled. This should seem rather strange because nearly every physical need in our life is easily accessible. We never have to worry if the weather will be too cold or too hot, because we have machines that can control the weather in our house. We don't have to worry if it's too dark to do something, because we have machines that control light. We never have to worry about preparing meals because there are drive-through windows on every corner and microwaves in every home. Pardon the subject matter, but we don't even have to worry about the female menstrual cycle, because that too can be controlled with the right technology. In fact, our tools allow us to control nearly all of the natural cycles of life.

And yet, all of this control hasn't necessarily resulted in more happiness for those who wield it. In his book *Technology and the Character of Contemporary Life*, philosopher Albert Borgmann identified something he called "the device paradigm," which works silently to enable this fast-paced and yet unsatisfying world.[12]

For Borgmann, a "device" is not just a mechanical or electronic gadget. Instead, he uses the word "device" to refer to a tool whose function takes a long, difficult process for a human and makes it available at the press of a button or the flip of a switch. For example, 150 years ago heating a home required going outside, finding trees, cutting them down, chopping the wood, bringing the wood inside, and starting a fire in the fireplace. This process would take significant time, and keeping the fire going would require skill and practice. But today, the commodity of heat is available at the press of a button through a device. Most of us don't think about where it comes from or how it works, because even a child can operate a thermostat.

Of course, Borgmann would say that this readily available heat is a good thing that often saves lives. But he points out that the device is also doing something that we don't notice—it is hiding the process of making heat. We press a button and heat comes out, but we don't know what goes on inside our walls or underneath our houses, and we no longer go about the practice of making heat ourselves. But why does this matter?

The answer is that when a device hides a process, sometimes we lose out on an important part of human life.

I encountered this firsthand when I first moved to Dallas several years ago. Some friends invited me to live with them in a hundred-year-old historical house with a beautiful porch around three sides of its structure. My roommates and I always talked about how great it would be to just sit out on the porch and hang out together, but we never really found the time. One day I ran into a man who was renovating one of the historic homes, and he told me that back when these houses were first built, everyone in the neighborhood used to be out on their porches. On hot summer afternoons, families would sit out on the porch, letting the breeze cool them off as they drank lemonade and shared stories about the day.

I told him I thought it was sad that people in the neighborhood never came out anymore, and I asked him if there had been some major conflict that made everyone go back inside. No, he said, it wasn't any conflict. What happened was that everyone installed air conditioners in their homes. Once cool air was available at the press of a button, they no longer needed to go outside to cool off. The device had hidden the process of cooling that used to take place outside, and the result was that the space where people used to commune became obsolete. Over time, as people spent more time indoors, neighbors become strangers.

Borgmann's point is not to say that we should get rid of our heating or cooling, but that we should be careful to notice the processes and practices that our devices hide and the humanity that is sometimes lost at the same time. Take, for example, meal preparation. There was a day when preparing lasagna meant spending all day making noodles, mixing the sauce, grinding the meat, and so on. Today, I can pull a Stouffer's lasagna out of the freezer, throw it in the oven, and have it ready a few minutes later. If I don't have time to wait for it to cook, I can always buy lasagna from a drive-through window and eat it in the car on the way to wherever I'm going.

The device paradigm is operating here because both the process of preparing a meal and the practice of eating it together at the table have been compressed down into what we call "fast food." Again, the point is not that fast food is inherently bad (although that might be true); the point is that, in compressing these human practices down into a commodity available at the press of a button, the space for human connection and depth is often lost. Imagine if the resurrected Jesus handed Peter a Big Mac and said, "You're all good. Get to it, buddy."

Borgmann, though, does not think the proper response to the device paradigm is to turn off our heaters or throw out our microwaves. Instead, he recommends that we take time to intentionally establish what he called "focal things and practices." These are things that might normally be hidden or made unnecessary by a device, but that we choose do anyway because of the kind of life we value.

For example, our cars, motorcycles, and Segways make walking or running long distances completely unnecessary. Yet, the practice of running a long distance keeps our bodies healthy and can bring calm to our hectic lives. In the language of Genesis, running helps us balance our "cultivating" of the garden with our "keeping" of it and helps restore the equilibrium between natural and unnatural.

Borgmann also concentrates his writing on the practice of the "Table" found in the New Testament. Fundamental to the life of the early church was the preparation and sharing of a meal. The table itself became a "focal thing," a place around which people gathered to share life and encourage each other in faith. Instead of living our lives according to the values of new technology, Borgmann urges us to determine what our values are first and attempt to use our tools in service of those values.

My wife and I recently attempted to do this in a small way that has had a big impact on our lives. When we first married, we bought a beautiful eight-person bar table for our home. Everyone who came over commented on how great it looked in our dining room. Unfortunately, it wasn't very comfortable and we found ourselves spending very little time there. As our family grew, we had trouble establishing mealtime as an important part of our lives. So recently, we decided to sell the pretty table for a more functional and comfortable one that we can sit at for hours with our children and friends. We did this because we have chosen to place a high value on the time we spend together, and although our technological culture urges us to go faster and faster, we work against those values every time we intentionally gather around the table as a focal thing.

As we grow older, I hope that our table functions the same way that Jesus' postresurrection breakfast did. Jesus intentionally used the practice of sharing a meal as the place where he would restore Peter and prepare him to be the leader of the church. This kind of intentionality will become even more important as we enter into the digital age. And that is where we will now turn.

VIRTUALIZATION

One evening this past summer, my friend Trey and I were talking in the church parking lot, and he asked me how long I thought it would take to read the Bible straight through. I wasn't sure, but told him that I remembered hearing estimates that if you read for about ten minutes a day, you'd finish the Bible in a year. When I got home, I decided to fire up a Bible database to calculate an exact number, and because I'm a web programmer I decided to turn my calculator into a simple website called www.howlongdoesittaketoreadthebible.com. Once it was up and running, I posted links to it on Twitter and Facebook, and within a few hours several friends reposted the link on their blogs and favorite social media sites. Within a day or two, several thousand people had visited the site and probably started to feel a bit guilty for not keeping up with their last Bible reading program.

This little story illustrates why I love being a part of Internet culture and feel blessed to be working in the web development world. The ability to instantly share information and create things that people all over the world can use is, in part, why this is a very interesting time in which to live. At the same time, however, if what we've been saying up to this point is correct, then we should expect that the Internet and its related technology also bring a set of tendencies and a distinct value system that may at times be in conflict with what we value as Christians.

If the Internet is a technology, then we should assume that it will present us with powerful new ways to shape the world, but that same power will also shape us and the way we see the world. If used without reflection, that shaping will eventually make its way into our souls, influencing how we see ourselves and others and what we think is important. Many of these effects will be rather innocuous, but we should never underestimate the capacity of our flesh to find ways to use technology for self-serving ends and as a means of distraction from our deep need for a Savior and his Body, the Christian community.

In order to help us think through the digital age, we will begin by reviewing the technologies that have come together to form the Internet. Once we've done this, we'll take a look at some of the ways these technologies shape us as individuals and communities, and then offer some recommendations on how to live faithfully in this era.

Book + Photograph + Telegraph + Telephone = Internet

The Internet and all of the devices we use to connect to it can be understood as the convergence of several older technologies. Books, radios, and telephones were distinct technologies with recognizable differences, but the Internet combines each of these mediums into one massive new system that can be difficult to comprehend. I have personally found it helpful to break the Internet down into the older technologies that have converged to create it and attempt to understand how those parts work together.

As a brief review, we said that the book as a medium values logical, linear, structured data sharing; and we saw that the print era was characterized by this kind of thinking. The medium of images, however, encourages a completely different way of thinking. Instead of valuing the abstract and the theoretical-like text, an image represents a particular point in time. Instead of being cognitively oriented like books, images tend to evoke emotional responses. When we think about our current image-saturated culture, we find that people often care more about how they feel about something than whether it is logically correct or morally right. This betrays a shift in our culture from thinking primarily through the medium of books to the medium of images. Just as the book and its related technologies coincided with the shift from "premodern" to "modern" thinking, the shift toward images has coincided with the shift toward a "postmodern" way of conceiving of the world.

Alongside the photograph came the telegraph, whose primary effect was to level information access. Before the telegraph, a person only had access to information that was physically nearby. People knew what was happening with their neighbors and in their village, but it would take days or months to hear about things happening farther away. The telegraph did away with these physical limitations to information. It transformed the world of information so that every person essentially had equal access to anything that happened, whether it was one house over or one continent over.

The telephone built upon the power of the telegraph, but instead of connecting people to distant information, the phone connected one person to another. Writing had long allowed people to communicate across physical distances, but a letter requires that the act of writing and the act of reading happen at different times. In contrast, the phone requires that speaking and hearing happen at the same time.

These four technological mediums—print, image, telegraph, and telephone—each uniquely transform an aspect of our lives. Print transforms our thinking, images transform our feeling, telegraphs transform our informing, and phones transform our relating. What do we get when we combine text, images, information access, and direct human-to-human connection? The answer is the most powerfully transformative technological system humans have ever created. The Internet and all of the websites, laptops, smartphones, tablets, and so on that we use to share information and connect to one another are now an essential part of our culture, and they both reflect and inform our values.

In chapter 6, we briefly mentioned Marshall McLuhan's idea that every technology functions to extend a natural human capacity. Part of what makes our connected systems so powerful is that they don't extend just one human function—they combine several of our human capacities into one device. This means that today's Internet-enabled smartphone is perhaps the most humanlike tool ever created. If one were to hazard a guess as to what technologies are coming in the future, it would be a safe bet that tomorrow's tools will be even more humanlike. If it is true that technology often functions as an idol of distraction, this means that today's technology can function as the most lifelike idol we have yet to create. But before we begin criticizing it, let us spend some time asking what kind of formation happens when we use these tools.

The Internet-Connected Soul

In contrast to the shovel we've continually referred to as having the capacity to physically reshape its user, our digital tools are not concerned with the physical world. Instead, because they are concerned with information, we should expect them to augment, extend, and transform the mind and heart of the user. We can see this happening by looking at three things our modern digital tools tend to value: access, speed, and interruption.

Access. By now, we've all experienced the incredible power of the Internet to allow us to instantly find information that would have taken days or weeks to acquire without a computer. The Internet was designed so that anyone can publish information with relative ease and very low cost, and it enables us to find that information with little effort. Like the printing press five hundred years before, the Internet has made it much more difficult for governments to suppress information or censor an individual's ability to publish something. Resources on everything from building a homemade radio to biblical apologetics make the Internet an incredible source of knowledge. I spend most of my days building tools for this world such as bestcommentaries.com, which aggregates scholarly ratings of biblical commentaries and is now used by thousands of pastors and students every week as they prepare lessons and sermons.

There are, however, several downsides—or trade-offs—that come with information access. The first is that we have access to the worst things humanity has to offer. As it has become popular to say, "our work machines and our porn machines are now *the same machines.*"[1] Computers and the Internet blur the lines between medium and content, and now the same computer that a child uses to learn math or biblical history is now capable of bringing him images and words that cause incredible damage to his soul.

A second downside to Internet information is that with equal access to all of the world's information, we tend to cultivate the skill of searching for and accessing information rather than acquiring information, committing it to memory, and allowing it to shape our minds and hearts. Tim Challies writes, "As we increasingly dedicate ourselves to the pursuit of information, we grow increasingly unable or unwilling to distinguish between knowledge and information."[2] If all we do is access information rather than acquire it, then our capacity for true wisdom is diminished.

Moreover, when we spend all of our time scanning and accessing information, we often find ourselves suffering from "information overload." But this is not just a feeling we have about too much data. Scientists at Temple University have shown that when we surround ourselves with many different pieces of information, our prefrontal cortex (the part of our brain that makes decisions) simply shuts off. Information is often helpful in making good decisions, but "with too much information people's decisions make less and less sense."[3] This has profound implications both for business and for the spiritual life.

Finally, along with great access to information comes an increased ability for everyone to "publish" anything, with little resistance or feedback. In many wonderful cases this allows people who wouldn't ordinarily be heard to have a voice. Yet, the ability to publish one's thoughts without any difficulty has the capacity to inflate our own ability and allows us to say things we might later regret. And this brings us to another important facet of modern communication tools: speed.

Speed. As a web developer, part of my job is to know that people look at and read text on the Internet differently than they read a book. When we use the technology of the book, we read text word by word and line by line. Once it's in our hands, we've to some extent committed to it, so we follow through with the act of reading. But when we read on a screen, we are almost always doing so in the context of looking for information. Our tendency is to scan headings and paragraphs looking for elements of interest, not to read word by word and line by line. If a page is not interesting or relevant, most people move on very quickly.

To give you a sense of how often we scan the Internet, I ran some numbers on how much content a popular blog produces. I surveyed the blog TechCrunch and found that on average, its writers produce about 2 million words a year. By comparison, that's around five times as many words as are in the entire Bible. Now TechCrunch has millions of readers, but I would guess that very few of them would say they have time to read the Bible five times every year. Yet they keep up with TechCrunch every day. Why are they able to read that blog but not the Bible? The answer is that they don't *read* TechCrunch; they *scan* it.[4]

Over time, as we cultivate the skill of scanning screens, many of us now find it more difficult to read a book word by word and line by line. Like a marathon runner who can't bench-press three hundred pounds, or a person who can bench-press three hundred pounds but can't run a marathon, we seem to cultivate either the skill of deep reading or the skill of scanning. It's possible to do both, but it is difficult to maintain both abilities. In an interview on PBS's *Charlie Rose Show*, Google's then CEO Eric Schmidt publicly worried about the effect this kind of reading—and the Internet as a whole—has:

> I worry that the level of interrupt, the sort of overwhelm-
> ing rapidity of information—and especially of stressful
> information—is in fact affecting cognition. It is in fact

affecting deeper thinking. I still believe that sitting down
and reading a book is the best way to really learn something. And I worry that we're losing that.

Interruption. Schmidt's concern leads us to a third major value of the Internet
age: interruption. Most of our tools are designed to inform us when important information is available. Phones ring when someone calls, and they
beep when we receive a text or an email. Computers alert us when software
updates are available, when our batteries run low, when we've misspelled a
word, and on and on. In a study from way back in 2004, researchers found
that information workers were interrupted to switch tasks on average every
three minutes.[5] This allows little time for workers to get into "the zone,"
but it also makes person-to-person connection extremely difficult. It is not
uncommon today to see several people sitting together at a restaurant or coffee shop, each distracted with something a device is telling them.

This brings us to the reasons why access, speed, and interruption are
important for Christians. A good portion of the Christian life requires the
ability to concentrate and focus on ideas over long periods of time. Spiritual
depth requires the ability to pray for more than a few minutes, to read and
memorize Scripture (not search for it online), and to love God with our
hearts *and* our minds. This means that we must be careful to cultivate and
retain the skill of deeply reading and deeply contemplating the things of
God, something the Internet and digital technologies do not value. We cannot read deeply when we spend all of our time scanning or when we allow
distraction to rule our minds.

The values of information access, speed, and interruption are not themselves morally wrong, but in a sinful world our tendency is toward compli-
cation, distraction, and chaos rather than simplicity, contemplation, and
order. We have to work against these tendencies in order to maintain balance between the natural and the unnatural in our lives.

The age before the Internet may offer us some clues as to how to do this.
In the previous chapter we saw how advances in manufacturing elevated
the values of mass consumption, materialism, and consumerism. Christians

living in this culture have had to learn to work against the value of accumulating possessions even as manufacturing technology engenders a desire for more.

Industrialization also brought two other important changes that we are just beginning to deal with—sedentary work environments and an abundance of food. Now that machines have freed people from doing physical labor, the majority of us now work at desks. At the same time food has become so plentiful that we are now faced with an obesity epidemic. Americans have unprecedented access to the healthiest food in the world, but we tend to eat unhealthy things because it is easier to access and faster to consume. In response, we've had to create concepts like "aerobics,"[6] and an entire industry of diet and exercise has sprung up to help us counteract the effects of overindulging in the benefits of industrialization. Perhaps our children will create gyms designed to strengthen their minds just as we created gyms to strengthen our bodies.

Until then, we who live in the age of information abundance will need to find ways to balance the amount, kind, and quality of the information we ingest. When we use the Internet and mobile devices, we drift toward what can be accessed quickly and consumed even faster. For those of us who want to cultivate a deep, spiritual life, we will have to be more selective in our information consumption and the media through which we consume it.

But the Internet today is not just about information consumption, it's about connecting people together with the newer technologies known as "social media." That title is rather interesting because it acknowledges that something social is occurring, but by definition that interaction takes place through a technological medium. How then does the medium affect the social?

Media-Mediated Community

I use the word "community" intentionally in the title above because when people, Christians in particular, discuss the online world, one of the first questions they ask is, "Is online community *real* community?" Those under thirty tend to answer yes, while those over thirty often say that "online" and "community" don't even make sense in the same sentence. But as with other technologies we've looked at, our goal in answering these questions is to observe the tendencies of behavior built into social media, figure out what values emerge out of those patterns, and then carefully consider where those do and do not align with what is important to the Christian life.

The social media landscape changes constantly, and as I write this new sites are coming online and the older ones are changing and adding new features. But even with this constant flux, we can make some generalizations about all of them. First, like the telephone, the function of social media is to connect physically distant people. But any time people are connected through a medium, that connection happens within the rules of the medium. Our question then should not be "Is it *real?*" because connecting online is just as "real" as talking on the phone or sending a letter. The better question is, what are the rules of the medium and what are the underlying messages and patterns that emerge from those rules?

Identity. Let's take a step back and consider what happens when someone uses a social networking website like Facebook. The first thing you have to do is create an account and fill out a profile. For the Internet generation, creating a profile is so common we rarely think about what we are doing, but if we look more closely at a profile page, we will notice some peculiar things that reflect what it values. First, before we can connect with someone else, we have to say something about ourselves. And we have to say those things within the boxes that Facebook has defined for us. For example, Facebook puts "Religion" and "Political View" next to each other and asks you to define both of them. In a face-to-face interaction, people rarely choose to lead with their political and religious views, much less link them together, but a Facebook profile transforms your identity into one that fits within its framework. When we use an online service like Facebook, we are, in effect, taking our identity and pushing it through that medium. Like meat put through a sausage grinder, what comes out on the other end is both like and unlike what we started with.

As we continue to fill out our profiles, add pictures, quotes, and favorite music, we are creating an identity that is closer to the "real" us and yet still not truly us. We then use that identity to interact with other people who have gone through a similar identity-shaping process. In a recent study conducted by the Girl Scouts of America, 74 percent of girls surveyed said that girls use social networking sites to seem "cooler than they really are." Girls who said they have low self-esteem were more likely than other girls to portray themselves as "sexy" or "crazy" in their profile.[7] Children with low self-esteem have always found ways to act out, but never before have they been connected to so many others who might take advantage of them. Even those of us who don't intentionally portray ourselves differently online can easily forget that when we go online we are in some sense *Alone Together* as the title of MIT professor Sherry Turkle's book suggests.[8]

Presence. When we move from creating a profile to interacting with others, we do so through the activities the system defines for us such as posting status updates, uploading photos, and commenting on other people's content. This allows old friends who now find themselves physically distant from one another to keep up with what's going on in each other's lives. Blogger and web developer Leisa Reichelt uses the term "ambient intimacy" to describe this background connection. She writes, "Ambient intimacy is about being able to keep in touch with people with a level of regularity and intimacy that you wouldn't usually have access to, because time and space conspire to make it impossible."[9] The Industrial Revolution created a world where we are no longer able to see our friends regularly, but online tools allow us to restore some of the day-to-day connection we've lost. As Sigmund Freud wrote almost a century ago, "If there had been no railway to conquer distance, my child would never have left town and I should need no telephone to hear his voice."[10]

In order to achieve ambient intimacy, friends need to continually post things about themselves—what they are thinking, feeling, and doing—for their friends to read about. To maintain this pattern, we have to regularly think about what we're thinking, feeling, and doing and then decide which of those things to communicate. In other words, when we do community online we have to think about ourselves much more than when we do community offline. Unlike simply being in a room with another person, being online with someone requires that we write, post, or say something to declare our presence. Matthew Anderson writes, "We cannot simply *be* online and influence others like we can be in a concert hall or with a friend and have influence. . . . [Online presence requires a person to] act intentionally in some way . . . through writing comments or linking or posting a video response."[11] Also, when we read online and interact textually, it is usually easier to be critical than it is to be constructive. It's difficult to say, "Good point," without sounding trite, but it's quick and easy to point out a problem.

Not only are our personal interactions shaped through online mediums, but even the way we begin and end relationships happens through a technological metaphor. Unlike offline friendships forged through shared experiences, time, and commitment, online friendships begin and end with a click of a button. Certainly many of our online friends are those we first met offline, but online it is possible to begin a relationship without ever meeting a person. I, like many in my generation, have cultivated deep friendships with those whom I originally met online and only later met in person. But that first meeting always has an initial awkwardness as both people attempt to find out how close the embodied person in front of us matches the disembodied person with whom we interacted online. These encounters have made me aware of the need to accurately present myself online. Am I presenting a person who I think of as better than who I truly am? And yet, even as I ask this question, I am engaging in more and more self-reflection.

Self-Orientation. This feedback loop of thinking about oneself is why many people conclude that the Internet makes us narcissistic. The word *narcissistic* comes from the Greek legend of Narcissus who was so enamored with his own beauty that the gods gave him the curse of spending the rest of his life looking at his own reflection in a mirror. When we interact online, we are forced to do the same. Every time we post anything online, tools like Facebook require us to watch ourselves do it. When I comment on a friend's

Facebook post, I immediately see a photo of myself saying the words. Even when I merely log in to read what others have said, I am immediately confronted with a picture of myself. When we go online, we tend to think that we're looking through a window into the lives of our friends, but, like an actual window, this one always shows us a reflection of ourselves before it shows us what's inside.

Of course, not everything we share online has to be about ourselves. The example at the beginning of the chapter, of my creating a simple web tool that I could share with others quickly and efficiently, is a powerful and fun use of the Internet. People can share Bible verses, stories of God's faithfulness, and common ministry interests in ways that no previous generation could. But another facet of online interaction is that all of it is recorded and counted.

When I posted www.howlongdoesittaketoreadthebible.com, I added some tracking code to count how many hits it received. Website tracking values numbers and statistics, which can be helpful in many situations. But in our fallenness we are always tempted to take something useful and twist it to fit our self-interests. It would be very easy for me to use the website tracker as a means to inflate my self-image. Second Samuel 24 (and 1 Chronicles 21) tells the story of when David commanded that the people and armies of Israel be counted. God severely rebuked David for doing this, not because counting itself is a sin, but because God recognized that David was using the census to flatter his own pride and lessen his dependence and trust in God.

But what was once available only to kings is now available to all of us. At any moment we can get up-to-date statistics on our fans, friends, and followers. Again, the statistics themselves are not sinful. The problem is that the more we use it, the more tempted we are to value what the technology values—numbers—over what the Scriptures would have us value.

As far back as Cain's city, we've said that our flesh will do whatever it can to make technology an idol of distraction. In the online world, the great danger is that we are constructing an idol of ourselves and becoming distracted with our own beauty. Like Narcissus we may become trapped in a feedback loop of looking at ourselves, but never seeing beneath the surface to the deeper sickness that can only be healed in an embodied community of faith. We are continually tempted to construct a Tower of Babel unto ourselves rather than work together on being the people of God, conformed into the image of his Son.

Working Through and Against Online Media

All of these problems might lead one to assume that the answer is to avoid social media and the Internet altogether. But that's not what I'm proposing here. We are attempting to balance the obvious usefulness of our tools with the knowledge of their inherent (sometimes positive, sometimes negative) value system so we can work both through their strengths and also against their weaknesses. Those born into Internet culture and those who feel comfortable in it will need to spend more time challenging it in order to avoid subtly giving in to its negative tendencies. On the flip side, those born earlier who find themselves uncomfortable in Internet culture may need to ask God to help them to avoid self-righteously running way from Internet culture like Jonah avoiding the Ninevites.

In chapter 1, we mentioned the apostle John's view of technology found in 2 John 12 where he wrote, "Though I have much to write to you, I would rather not use paper and ink. Instead I hope to come to you and talk face to face, so that our joy may be complete."

John was comfortable using the communication technology—pen and ink—of his day, but he did so with a set of values that were contrary to the tendencies built into the technology of writing. Whereas a letter requires that one isolated person write a message and then another isolated person later read that message, John says that his joy is never complete until he is physically present with his community. And yet, aware of this problem, John used writing because he understood both its helpfulness and its problematic value system. From that perspective he was able to use technology in service of the embodied communal life that Christ taught him.

When John could not be physically present with his community, he was comfortable using technology to communicate with them. But he was always careful to state that he considered technologically mediated relationships to be inferior to embodied relationships. For John, both embodied and disembodied communication were "real"; he simply believed that only face-to-face reality offered him "complete joy."

The great temptation of the digital generation is to inadvertently disagree with John and assume that online presence offers the same kind of "complete joy" as offline presence. Our problem is not that technologically mediated relationships are unreal, nor is the problem that all online communication is self-focused and narcissistic. Rather, the danger is that just like the abundance of food causes us to mistake sweet food for nourishing food, and just like the abundance of information can drown out deep thinking, the abundance of virtual connection can drown out the kind of life-giving, table-oriented life that Jesus cultivated among his disciples. Social media follows the device paradigm in that it masks the long, sometimes arduous process of friendship and makes it available at the press of a button.

Yet, just because social media follows the device paradigm does not mean that we should abandon it any more than we should abandon air-conditioning. Though such speculation is rarely useful, we can only assume that if the apostles were alive today, they would continue using the technology of the day. Yet, as John modeled for us, they would do so with their value system in mind, always seeking to use technology in service of embodied life, not as a replacement for embodied life.

A second great temptation for those of us who desire embodied life is that mobile technology allows us to coexist in both the online and offline worlds at the same time. As we commune with friends and family and share meals together, the online world is always close at hand with statistics, numbers, and interaction. The people in front of us might be sick, moody, unfriendly, or in need of a diaper change. But there is no "unfriend" or "unparent" button for those difficult situations, and this makes it all the more tempting to sneak away to a world of constant interaction and adulation. The people on our phones are beautiful and interesting, and we can ignore them when they are not. However, the world in our pockets doesn't give out rewards for faithfulness and long-suffering, only for the moment-by-moment interactions it requires, urging us to return and return again for a fleeting feeling of connection.

But we followers of Jesus do value faithfulness, and we do value staying in a relationship even when "it's complicated."[12] This means that if we are to exist in the online world, we must both work through it, but also at times work against some of what it values. Social media enables all kinds of good and helpful interaction; people raise money for orphanages and share helpful links with one another. But as we interact via social media, we must remember that those interactions do not offer the "complete joy" that comes from the kind of embodied faithfulness that Jesus modeled for us.

In our family, we've attempted to take practical steps to foster the kind of relational world that Jesus and his disciples had. When I come home from work around 5:00 PM, I've decided to put my phone and computer away until I put my kids to bed at 7:30 PM; and my wife does the same with her computer and phone. This serves to carve out of the day a space (or as Borgmann calls it, a "focal place") where we can interact together and share meals as a family. As my kids grow older, we plan to do this together as a family, with all of us putting our devices together in a common basket. When we are all disconnected from the world out there, it frees us up to be fully present with the people right here in front of us. When I go back to work, I spend my day on the Internet interacting with people and building websites, but I attempt to do so for the purpose of fostering embodied life, not replacing it. At home, I try to use technology to create focal space for our family to grow, and at work I create technology that helps others do the same.

The guiding principle is this: technology is for the table. This doesn't mean that technology and the table are in opposition, only that everything we do with our tools—scheduling appointments on our phones, heating up meals in the microwave, reading updates from friends and family on social networks—should all be directed toward enriching the few, precious face-to-face encounters we have in our busy world. Here's a simple example of how this might work: pull out your phone, schedule an appointment with a friend you haven't seen in a while, and in the meantime carefully observe what he or she is saying online. When you do meet, you won't have to spend as much time getting updated on what's happened since the last time you were together, allowing you to move more easily into deeper communion with one another. Used in this way, your calendar and social network technology are directed toward the table, and hopefully they will increase your chances of experiencing the "complete joy" that John wanted to have with his fellow believers.

I wish I could say that I do this every time I meet with people. And I wish I could say every evening between 5:00 PM and 7:30 PM is the best time of my life where flowers bloom and my kids always behave. But marriage, parenting, and friendships can be difficult at times, and often I would rather check my stats and see how many people have congratulated me online for something I made or said. But I don't like the person I become when I spend all my time online any more than the person I become when I spend all of my time eating McDonald's food. Instead, I know that it is often the difficult things—eating healthy food and exercising, reading books for long periods, praying deeply, and spending quality time with my family and friends—that God uses to mold and shape us into the image of his Son. Rather than be shaped by technology, I try to understand how each new technology can shape me and then decide if that coincides with the kind of person I think God would have me be.

RECOMMENDATIONS

If I've been successful in this book, I will have convinced you that technology changes everything. This is because the nature of technology is to *transform*. God has charged us with the responsibility to cultivate and keep his garden, and we use tools to fulfill that command. But the tools we use not only transform God's creation, they also transform us. From the shovel that reshapes our hands, arms, and minds to the mobile phone that modifies our conception of space, friendship, and wilderness, every tool shapes the world and reshapes it user. In addition, our tools are powerful conveyers of meaning and values that have the capacity to shape the soul.

According to the biblical story, we live in the time between the Garden and the City, anticipating Christ's return when he will make all things new—including our souls, our bodies, our planet, and even some of the things we've made. We recognize that technology has a powerful yet limited redemptive capacity, but that it also has corruptive tendencies. How then should the Christian live in a technological age? How can we "seek the welfare of the city" (Jer. 29:7) without giving in to its downsides?

One approach is to avoid all new technology and attempt to go as far backward in time as possible to the age when things seemed to be simpler and better. While this approach is at times tempting, we must remember that we've not been called to go backward in time but to live faithfully in our own age. At the other extreme, we might argue that we should use technology as much and as often as we can, not worrying about its problems because at Christ's return he will remake all things, including our problematic technology. But this forward-looking approach will similarly fail the test of living faithfully with what we've been given.

At the conclusion of his book, David Hopper writes, "The challenge to theology of technology's coming of age is for theology to affirm its own proper counterproject of life-in-community. . . . It must speak from isness and not . . . from the perspective of some 'final hope.'"[1] Hopper is saying that Christians cannot be content merely to criticize technology on the one hand, nor to simply look toward Christ's return on the other. Instead, the Christian community must begin from what God has called it to be—its "isness"—and live out of that. Only from that position can we faithfully approach and cautiously use technology. To see how this might practically work out, I would recommend five steps: valuation, experimentation, limitation, togetherness, and cultivation.

Valuation. We must begin by continually returning to the Scriptures to find our Christian values and identity. From that perspective we can evaluate the strengths and weaknesses of technology and determine what values will emerge from the tendencies of use built into its design. In the appendix you'll find a set of questions based on what we learned from the biblical story. This is designed to help surface these patterns and emergent values. After going through this evaluation process, we can ask where our Christian values and the values of technology might be in conflict, and what aspects of the tool our flesh will be tempted to use in ways that do not honor God.

For example, the New Testament repeatedly affirms the fullness and completeness that only comes through embodied face-to-face interaction. Mobile phones, however, can only enable disembodied communication, and they tend to value being connected to those who are physically absent rather than those who are nearby. Mobile phones are still helpful and useful, but in order to have the fullness of Christian community, we must work both through and against the value system of the phone.

Experimentation. Thinking about technology is helpful, but it's difficult to discover the tendencies and value systems built into a technology without actually using it. A controlled experiment in using a tool can help us discover things that we can only know through experience. For example, I tried making a newspaper my only source of news for two weeks. Instead of watching TV, listening to the radio, or using the Internet, I bought a paper every day for two weeks. The differences were staggering. I found that I treated news differently when I paid for it. I found myself exposed to stories that I normally wouldn't have seen. I also found it difficult to take a "news break" at work since everyone could see me pull out the newspaper, whereas no one noticed when I opened up a browser tab to a news website.

A church, for example, could intentionally experiment with the amount of media, the size of their band, the lighting in the room, and so on, carefully noting what differences in meaning emerged. Individuals can try things like hand-writing notes to friends, and someone not familiar with texting or Twitter could try it for several weeks to discover what it means to use it. Although one does not necessarily have to use a technology to understand it, a good experiment can do something even more important—it can help a person from one techno-culture understand the people who live in another techno-culture.

Limitation. Once we understand the patterns of usage of a technology, the next step is to see what happens when we put boundaries on it. If we become convinced that spending too much time on social media sites invites narcissism and that reading online limits deep thinking, then a disciplined set of limits is necessary. It is here that the desires of the flesh often emerge most strongly. A person who checks his or her mobile phone regularly throughout the day may find it extremely difficult to curtail this pattern.

Because of this difficulty, incorporating a "technology fast" into one's diet can be particularly helpful. It is, of course, somewhat misleading to call it a "fast" since we're still using twentieth-century tools like lights, air-conditioning, and vehicles; but choosing to abstain for several days from the tools that impact us most powerfully can help weaken their control. In my profession, I've found it difficult to disconnect for several days at a time, so instead I try to make disconnection a regular part of every day. In the morning when I get up, I avoid checking email right away, and in the evening when I come home, I don't use the computer until the kids are in bed. My goal is not simply to limit my technology usage but to open up space to live the kind of life that Christ modeled for us. When I feel the urge to go outside of these boundaries, I have to ask myself if I'm doing so out of my Christian values and identity, or if I'm being pulled into the value system of technology.

Togetherness. The previous three steps—valuation, experimentation, and limitation—will be rendered mostly useless if we practice them in isolation apart from the context of Christian fellowship. An interesting example of making community-based technology decisions can be found in Eric Brende's book *Better Off* in which he describes living for eighteen months in a small, technologically minimalist community very similar to an Amish village. In one story the entire community came together to discuss the pros and cons of installing a single phone in their midst.[2] Another very high profile example of a group-oriented technology decision came in 2010, when the trapped Chilean miners decided as a group not to allow personal music players or video games because they determined that "those tend to isolate people from one another."[3]

Today's technology places a high value on personalization, customization, and the preferences of the individual. That makes the decision of the Chilean miners to value the needs of the group over the desires of the individuals a radical departure from the value system of technological society. Anytime we choose to do technology together rather than as individuals, we are rejecting the self-centered orientation of the flesh and choosing to work out the togetherness portrayed in the Scripture and within the triune God.

Cultivation. Finally, in our attempts to approach technology with discernment, we must be careful not to enter into a kind of inactive stasis where we talk about technology but fail to support those who are actually *doing* technology in service of what God has asked of his image bearers: to cultivate and keep his creation and to make disciples of all nations.

In recent years, Christian communities have been rediscovering the importance of cultivating and nurturing artists, and I think the time has come for us to begin doing the same with those working in technology. We already spend time and resources developing and encouraging business people and politicians, yet it is the technologists—the men and women creating the next generation of tools—who are often implicitly making important decisions about health care, energy, Internet regulation, privacy, weapons availability, biomedical advances, and so on. We are not all called to be inventors, but we can work toward helping technologists think theologically and Christianly about what they are making. I hope that this book is a helpful starting point for doing this.

If there is one final recommendation I can give in regard to technology, it is that we attempt to do something like what this book has done. We must continually attempt to view technology through the lens of the story of God and his people, with the resurrected Christ at beginning, middle, and end of that story. It is his life, work, and promises that should inform our value system, shape the way we see the world, and transform the way we live in it.

It is my hope that the biblical and philosophical tools presented in this book will help us become better stewards of the technological tools God has entrusted to us, as we seek to live lives that honor him and the work of his Son. And on our journey from the Garden to the City, I pray that we never confuse the city for the Savior.

TECHNOLOGY TETRAD

Below is the chart from chapter 9 that brings together the four parts of the biblical story—creation, fall, redemption, and restoration—in a way that allows us to consider positive, negative, intentional, and unintentional aspects of technology. After this chart, you'll find questions that you can ask in groups to help surface issues about any technology you might want to consider.

	Positive	Negative
Unintentional	1. Reflection	4. Restoration
Intentional	3. Redemption	2. Rebellion

Reflection

- What unique aspects of God's nature does this technology reflect?
- What aspects of our human nature does this technology enhance and extend?

- How does this technology help accomplish the creation mandate to cultivate the earth and create from it?
- Is this technology more practically oriented (used to accomplish a task), or does it exist for its own sake (to be beautiful)?
- Is this tool primarily used to create new things, or is it used primarily to consume things that exist?
- What patterns of behavior have emerged over time as this technology has taken hold in society?
- What actions, thoughts, and social structures does this technology value or favor?

Rebellion

- What obvious negative uses of this technology do you know of?
- What embedded values does this technology have that are in conflict with a biblical portrait of humanity?
- What aspects of this technology's power will our flesh be tempted to exploit (Gal. 5:17; James 1:13–15)?
- In what ways could this technology reinforce the myth that we can live apart from dependence upon God (Gen. 4:17)?
- What will happen if we use this technology too much (Eph. 5:18a)?
- What limits can we place on using this technology to prevent it from using us (Mark 9:43; Heb. 12:1)?

Redemption

- What effects of the fall can this technology help to overcome (Gen. 3:7; 1 Tim. 5:23)?
- Is this technology primarily designed for entertainment and fun (e.g., video games) or does it have a greater significance (e.g., cochlear implants)?
- What embedded values does this technology have that are a complement to the biblical image of humanity and the Church?

- How can this technology be used to accomplish Jesus' commands to help the less fortunate (Matt. 25:34–40)?
- How does this technology point toward the final redemption that Christ has promised?

Restoration

- What unintended consequences, shortcomings, or trade-offs does this technology bring?
- Is it possible to use the technology in a different way to avoid these problems? If not, how does the presence of such problems help us long for the future restoration of all things through Christ?
- Do the benefits of this technology outweigh its shortcomings?
- How do you imagine God would make this technology better in the new City?
- What creative ways can you contribute to making this technology better?

NOTES

Introduction

1. I invite you to visit www.donteatthefruit.com.

Chapter 1: Perspective

1. This quote is widely attributed to Alan Kay (sometimes in the alternate form, "technology is anything that wasn't around when you were born"), but no specific source has been provided. The closest reference I could find was possibly from a Hong Kong press conference in the 1980s.

2. To describe this phenomenon, Tom Pettitt coined the term "Gutenberg parenthesis" in a lecture given at the international conference of Media in Transition (April 2007). See "Before the Gutenberg Parenthesis: Elizabethan-American Compatibilities," http://web.mit.edu/comm-forum/mit5/papers/pettitt_plenary_gutenberg.pdf.

3. Arthur C. Clarke, "Hazards of Prophecy: The Failure of Imagination," in *Profiles of the Future: An Enquiry into the Limits of the Possible*, rev. ed. (New York: Henry Holt & Co, 1984), 36.

4. Jamais Cascio, "Your Posthumanism Is Boring Me," *io9.com*, May 8, 2010, http://io9.com/5533833/your-posthumanism-is-boring-me-.

5. Douglas Adams, "How to Stop Worrying and Learn to Love the Internet," September 1, 1999, http://www.douglasadams.com/dna/19990901-00-a.html.

6. Hilary Stout, "How Does Technology Affect Kids' Friendships?" *New York Times*, posted April 30, 2010 (print edition May 2, 2010), http://www.nytimes.com/2010/05/02/fashion/02BEST.html.

7. The plural of *medium* in this sense is usually *media*, which means that *mediums* is unconventional, if not outright grammatically incorrect. However, because the word

media is often associated with "news media" and "the media," I have opted for *mediums* as the plural of *medium*.

8. Martin Heidegger was a twentieth-century German philosopher whose controversial work, "The Question Concerning Technology" (available online at http://www.wright .edu/cola/Dept/PHL/Class/P.Internet/PITexts/QCT.html) was enormously influential in subsequent discussions concerning the nature of technology and being human in a technological world.

9. Other works go deeper into such issues. For example, Jack Swearengen, a former nuclear scientist, explored far-reaching implications of nuclear technology in *Beyond Paradise: Technology and the Kingdom of God* (Eugene, OR: Wipf and Stock, 2007); and Brian Brock offers a deeper look into the theology and philosophy of technology and offers guidance on applying it to modern issues in *Christian Ethics in a Technological Age* (Grand Rapids: Eerdmans, 2010).

10. Arthur Boers, *Living into Focus: Choosing What Matters in an Age of Distractions* (Ada, MI: Brazos, forthcoming 2012), chapter 5.

11. Thankfully, Socrates's student Plato recorded many of Socrates's best dialogues, preserving his thoughts for the ages. One of the stories Plato preserved for us is called *Phaedrus* in which Socrates shared his concerns about the written word. He did this by telling his students the legend of the Egyptian god Theuth who offered the gift of writing to King Thamus. Theuth believed writing would be a remedy for bad memories, but King Thamus objected, saying that the true result would be creating people who had only the appearance of wisdom.

Chapter 2: Imagination

1. David Nye, *Technology Matters: Questions to Live With* (Cambridge, MA: MIT Press, 2007), 3.

2. Egbert Schuurman, *Faith and Hope in Technology* (Toronto: Clements Publishing, 2003), 64–65.

3. David A. Mindell, "Cultural Impacts of Technology," *Wiley Encyclopedia of Electrical and Electronics Engineering*, ed. John G. Webster (Hoboken, NJ: John Wiley & Sons, 1999), 1, doi:10.1002/047134608X.W7301. Thanks to Dr. Merritt Roe Smith for helping me track this down.

4. For the use of the shovel as a metaphor for technology, I am indebted to Dr. T. David Gordon, author of *Why Johnny Can't Preach* (Phillipsburg, NJ: P & R Publishing, 2009), for telling me the following joke: "When I'm gardening and my wife asks me, 'What are you making?' I always answer, 'Blisters!'"

5. John Culkin, "A Schoolman's Guide to Marshall McLuhan," *Saturday Review*, March 18, 1967, 51.

6. Carr works through studies on the brain's "plasticity" in chapter 2 of *The Shallows: What the Internet Is Doing to Our Brains* (New York: W. W. Norton, 2010), 17–35.

7. Marshall McLuhan, *Understanding Media: The Extensions of Man* (Cambridge, MA: MIT Press, 1994), 7.

8. "Life Expectancy by Age, 1850–2004," Information Please Database, Pearson Education, Inc., 2007, http://www.infoplease.com/ipa/A0005140.html (accessed April 10, 2011).

9. By the year 2000, the world infant mortality rate was cut down to a third of what it was in 1950. It dropped from 153 deaths per 1,000 births to 52. In the United States,

there were only 6 deaths per 1,000 births in the year 2000. In contrast, prior to 1900 infant mortality rates could be as high as 1 in every 3 births. United Nations, Department of Economic and Social Affairs, Population Division, *World Population Prospects: The 2008 Revision*, New York, 2009 (advanced Excel tables), http://data.un.org/Data.aspx?d=PopDiv&f=variableID:77.

10. Kathleen McGowan, "Stone Age Technology," *Discover Presents: Origins*, summer 2010, 71 (a special edition of *Discover Magazine*, http://www.discovermagazine.com/).
11. David H. Hopper, *Technology, Theology, and the Idea of Progress* (Louisville, KY: Westminster/John Knox Press, 1991), 10.

Chapter 3: Reflection

1. Stanley James Grenz and John R. Franke, *Foundationalism: Shaping Theology in a Postmodern Context* (Louisville, KY: Westminster/John Knox Press, 2000), 141–46.
2. Emil Brunner, *Christianity and Civilization* (London: Nisbet, 1948), 62.
3. Andy Crouch, *Culture Making: Recovering Our Creative Calling* (Downers Grove, IL: InterVarsity Press, 2008), 23.
4. Lera Boroditsky, "How Does Our Language Shape the Way We Think?" In *What's Next: Dispatches on the Future of Science*, ed. Max Brockman (New York: Vintage, 2009), 127.
5. If you're interested in further discussion, this field of study is called "Speech Act Theory" and was pioneered by John Austin in the 1960s.

Chapter 4: Definition

1. Stephen J. Kline, "What Is Technology?" in *Philosophy of Technology: The Technological Condition: An Anthology*, ed. Robert C. Scharff and Val Dusek (Malden, MA: Blackwell, 2003), 210–12.
2. Neil Postman, *Technopoly: The Surrender of Culture to Technology* (New York: Alfred A. Knopf, 1992), 13.
3. At this point, I must express my deep indebtedness to Stephen V. Monsma's more nuanced definition of technology as "a distinct human cultural activity in which human beings exercise freedom and responsibility in response to God by forming and transforming the natural creation, with the aid of tools and procedures, for practical ends and purposes." *Responsible Technology*, by Stephen V. Monsma, Clifford Christians, Eugene R. Dykema, et al., ed. Stephen V. Monsma (Grand Rapids: Eerdmans, 1986), 19. Thanks to Tim Challies for working with me on shortening it. It only took twenty emails or so.

Chapter 5: Rebellion

1. Hebrew בָּרָא (*bara*): Gen. 1:1, 21, 27; 2:3, 4; 5:1, 2; 6:7.
2. Hebrew יָצַר (*yatsar*): Gen. 2:7, 8, 19.
3. Hebrew עָשָׂה (*asah*): Gen. 1:7, 11, 12, 16, 26, 26, 31; 2:2, 3, 4, 18; 3:1, 7, 14, 21.
4. Other translators argue that the text should read "garments *for* their skin" rather than "garments of skin." In either case, God is still creating.
5. Jacques Ellul, *The Meaning of the City*, trans. Dennis Pardee (Grand Rapids: Eerdmans, 1993), 11.
6. The idea that the city represents the best of human ingenuity can be seen in the title

of Edward Glaeser's book *Triumph of the City: How Our Greatest Invention Makes Us Richer, Smarter, Greener, Healthier, and Happier* (New York: Penguin, 2011).

7. From the Latin *incurvatus in se*. Saint Augustine, *Lectures on Romans* (Louisville: Westminster/John Knox Press, 2006), 1515–16.

8. Saint Augustine, *The City of God*, trans. Marcus Dods (New York: Modern Library, 2000), 14.13, p. 461.

9. Blaise Pascal, *Pensées* (Sioux Falls, SD: NuVision Publications, 2007), II:139, p. 39.

10. Again, we are not attempting to make the biblical story about the origin of tools and the culture map to any archaeological accounts. We are simply affirming that the Bible is truthful and allowing others to sort out the details.

Chapter 6: Approach

1. Marshall McLuhan, *Understanding Media: The Extensions of Man* (Cambridge, MA: MIT Press, 1994), 17–18.

2. Langdon Winner, *The Whale and the Reactor: A Search for Limits in an Age of High Technology* (Chicago: University of Chicago Press, 1988), 103.

3. Leo Marx, "Technology: The Emergence of a Hazardous Concept," *E-Technology and Culture: The International Quarterly of the Society for the History of Technology* 51, no. 2 (July 2010), http://etc.technologyandculture.net/2010/08/technology-a-hazardous-concept/.

4. Today, there is a new debate asking whether "online church" should be considered "real" community. It is easy to dismiss online church as incapable of offering any form of true community, yet we know that every medium (writing, phone, television, etc.) has some capacity for human connection. Instead of asking *if* online church brings community (which it certainly does), we would do better to ask *what kind* of community happens online and if it is sufficient for a normative gathering of the Body of Christ. It is clear that in situations when a person cannot attend a physical church (for medical, security, or geographic reasons) an online model is of tremendous benefit. But if 2 John 1:12 is our guide, then church that happens through a medium will never offer the "complete joy" of a face-to-face encounter and therefore should not be our normative way of meeting. However, this need for face-to-face interaction also applies to large churches in which it is possible to be near people, but never truly be face-to-face.

Chapter 7: Redemption

1. On December 30, 2009, twenty-nine-year-old David Matthews created a Facebook page asking *Saturday Night Live* (SNL) creator Lorne Michaels to invite Betty White to host SNL. By February 2010, the page had over 300,000 fans, and by March she was asked to host the show.

2. Exodus 20:3–5. Jews, Roman Catholics, and some Lutherans enumerate the Ten Commandments differently, putting these two commandments together. In either case, the following points are the same.

3. Neil Postman, *Amusing Ourselves to Death: Public Discourse in the Age of Show Business* (New York: Penguin, 1985), 9. Emphasis in the original.

Chapter 8: Mediums

1. See chapter 1, note 7.

2. Interestingly, when phones were first used, it was considered impolite to start a

conversation with "Hello." Our usage patterns and social conventions change over time as seen in Claude S. Fischer's book *America Calling: A Social History of the Telephone to 1940* (Berkeley: University of California Press, 1994).

3. Marc Prensky, "Digital Natives, Digital Immigrants," *On the Horizon* 9, no. 5 (October 2001), http://www.marcprensky.com/writing/Prensky%20-%20Digital%20Natives,%20Digital%20Immigrants%20-%20Part1.pdf.

4. For a more detailed analysis of changes in biblical interpretation, see Marshall McLuhan and Eric McLuhan, *Laws of Media: The New Science* (Toronto: University of Toronto Press, 1992), 218. Thanks to Joseph Kim for letting me see an early version of his dissertation, "Marshall McLuhan's Theological Anthropology," which will be published by Dallas Theological Seminary.

5. The Hebrew Old Testament actually had various numbering and organizing systems for quite some time before chapter and verse numbers were added to the Greek New Testament.

6. Shane Hipps, *Flickering Pixels: How Technology Shapes Your Faith* (Grand Rapids: Zondervan, 2009), 76.

7. For scientific quantification of how pornography uniquely interacts with the human brain, see William M. Struthers, *Wired for Intimacy: How Pornography Hijacks the Male Brain* (Downers Grove, IL: InterVarsity Press, 2009).

8. It's important to distinguish between the "icon" used in early Christian worship and the "images" we use today. Icons are deliberately unrealistic so that they can direct the viewer away from the icon itself and point toward a spiritual reality. In contrast, images are designed to be as realistic as possible. Eastern Orthodox worship permits icons, but not images, while Catholic worship requires images. Thanks to Dr. T. David Gordon for this distinction. The point I am making here is that the early church thought deeply about the theological meaning of the mediums they employed in worship.

9. St. John Damascene, *On Holy Images*, trans. Mary H. Allies (London: Thomas Baker, 1898); available at http://www.fordham.edu/halsall/basis/johndamascus-images.html.

Chapter 9: Restoration

1. Geoffrey A. Fowler, "Facebook's 'Social' Chief Pushes Human Interaction," *Wall Street Journal* online, October 10, 2010, http://online.wsj.com/article/SB100014240 52748704127904575544302659920236.html.

2. Some scholars have argued that, in reference to Joseph and Jesus, the word *tektōn* should be translated "stonemason" rather than "carpenter" because Jesus grew up in Nazareth at the time when the nearby city of Sepporus was being built. The main material in the region was stone instead of wood, and Sepporus was built from that stone, so its builders would have employed masons instead of carpenters.

Of course, there is no way to know for certain whether the kind of *tektōn* ("skilled work") that Joseph did was that of carpentry or masonry, but in either case Jesus' death involved woodwork and his resurrection involved stonework.

3. Jacques Ellul, *The Meaning of the City*, trans. Dennis Pardee (Grand Rapids: Eerdmans, 1993), 173.

4. Some passages in which the phrase "in person" or "face-to-face" are used are Acts 25:16; Rom. 1:11; 1 Cor. 13:12; 2 Cor. 10:1; Gal. 1:22; Col. 2:1; 1 Thess. 2:17; 3:10; 2 Tim. 1:4; 4:9; 2 John 12; 3 John 13–14.

Chapter 10: Technicism

1. The One Laptop Per Child (OLPC) project was created by Nicholas Negroponte to bring low-cost, networked laptops to children in impoverished countries with the hope that access to information and development of computer skills would contribute to solving problems in those countries.
2. Kevin Kelly, *What Technology Wants* (New York: Viking, 2010), 148.
3. Saint Augustine, *The City of God*, trans. Marcus Dods (New York: Modern Library, 2000), 14.28, p. 447.
4. Stephen V. Monsma, Clifford Christians, Eugene R. Dykema, et al., *Responsible Technology*, ed. Stephen V. Monsma (Grand Rapids: Eerdmans, 1986), 50.
5. Francis Bacon, *The New Organon* (Indianapolis: Bobbs-Merrill, 1960), 39; quoted in Monsma, *Responsible Technology*, 84.
6. Ray Kurzweil, "The Evolution of Mind in the Twenty-first Century," in *Are We Spiritual Machines? Ray Kurzweil vs. the Critics of Strong A.I.* (Seattle: Discovery Institute, 2002), 53.
7. Michael DeLashmutt attempted to ask this very question to several people in the information technology industry, but they did not openly use such terms to describe technology. DeLashmutt, "A Better Life Through Information Technology? The Posthuman Person in Contemporary Speculative Science," *Zygon* 41, no. 2 (2006): 267–88.
8. For a much more nuanced discussion of the connection between democracy, classical liberalism, and technology, see Murray Jardine's book *The Making and Unmaking of Technological Society* (Grand Rapids: Brazos, 2004).
9. Please don't misunderstand this as criticism of Apple or Apple products. I quite enjoy them, and in fact I wrote myself a reminder on my iPhone to add this note. I am only pointing out that the creators of the Apple logo were very explicit in portraying technology overcoming human fallenness. For a more detailed analysis of Apple's logo, see Andy Crouch, "A World Without Jobs," January 19, 2011, http://www.culture-making.com/articles/a_world_without_jobs.
10. "Productivity" is calculated by comparing the value of the goods workers produce to the value of the goods they consume during production. An infographic on the subject can be found at http://www.good.is/post/does-technology-make-us-more-productive-workers/.
11. Ruth Schwart Cowen, *More Work for Mother: The Ironies of Household Technology from the Open Hearth to the Microwave* (New York: Basic Books, 1985).
12. Albert Borgmann, *Technology and the Character of Contemporary Life: A Philosophical Inquiry*, chapter 9 (Chicago: University of Chicago Press, 1984), 40–47.

Chapter 11: Virtualization

1. The original source of this idea has been difficult to trace, but it did appear online in this article: Justin E. H. Smith, "On the Internet," in *Berfrois* [blog], January 7, 2011, http://www.berfrois.com/2011/01/on-the-Internet/.
2. Tim Challies, *The Next Story: Life and Faith After the Digital Explosion* (Grand Rapids: Zondervan, 2011), 199.
3. Sharon Begley, "I Can't Think!" *Newsweek*, February 27, 2011, http://www.newsweek.com/2011/02/27/i-can-t-think.html.

4. John Dyer, "Blogs vs. Classics: The New Experience of Language," *Don't Eat the Fruit* (blog), January 29, 2009, http://donteatthefruit.com/2009/01/blogs-vs-classics-the -new-experience-of-language/.
5. Victor M. González and Gloria Mark, "Constant, Constant, Multi-tasking Crazi- ness: Managing Multiple Working Spheres," Proceedings of ACM CHI'04: Confer- ence on Human Factors in Computing Systems (Vienna, Austria, April 26–29, 2004), 113–20.
6. It wasn't until 1968 that Kenneth H. Cooper coined the terms "aerobics" and "aerobic exercise" in his book *Aerobics* (New York: Bantam Books, 1968).
7. Girl Scout Research Institute, *"Who's That Girl?* Image and Social Media Survey" and *"Who's That Girl* factsheet" (New York: Girl Scouts of the USA, 2010), http://www .girlscouts.org/research/publications/stem/image_and_social_media_survey.asp.
8. Sherry Turkle, *Alone Together: Why We Expect More from Technology and Less from Each Other* (New York: Basic Books, 2011). Turkle has written many books on the positive aspects of social networks, but she says *Alone Together* was a kind of "repentance" for leaving out the more negative influences it can have. Also see Ira Flatow, "Have We Grown Too Fond of Technology?" *NPR*, February 25, 2011, http://www.npr.org /2011/02/25/134059283/have-we-grown-too-fond-of-technology.
9. Leisa Reichelt, "Ambient Intimacy," March 1, 2007 (blog), http://www.disambiguity .com/ambient-intimacy/.
10. Sigmund Freud, *Civilization and Its Discontents* (New York: W. W. Norton, 1961), 38.
11. Matthew Lee Anderson, "Three Cautions Among the Cheers: The Dangers of Uncriti- cally Embracing New Media" in *The New Media Frontier: Blogging, Vlogging, and Pod- casting for Christ*, ed. John Mark Reynolds and Roger Overton (Wheaton: Crossway, 2008), 63.
12. This is a reference to Facebook's "It's complicated" as a status for one's relationship to another person.

Recommendations

1. David H. Hopper, *Technology, Theology, and the Idea of Progress* (Louisville, KY: West- minster/John Knox Press, 1991), 113.
2. Eric Brende, *Better Off: Flipping the Switch on Technology* (New York: Harper Collins, 2005), 134ff.
3. MailOnline, "The tiny cage that will save their lives: Capsule built to hoist trapped Chilean miners up through 2,330ft of rock arrives," last updated September 27, 2010, http://www.dailymail.co.uk/news/article-1315342/Trapped-Chilean-miners-cage -built-hoist-2-330ft-rock.html.

INDEX

ABOUT THE AUTHOR

John Dyer (ThM, Dallas Theological Seminary) has been a web developer for more than ten years, building tools for Apple, Microsoft, Harley Davidson, and the Department of Defense. He currently serves as the Director of Web Development for Dallas Theological Seminary and lives near Dallas, Texas, with his wife, Amber, and two children, Benjamin and Rebecca. He has written on technology and faith for *Christianity Today* and *Collide Magazine*. *From the Garden to the City* is his first book (www .fromthegardentothecity.com). You can find out more about his coding and writing at http://j.hn/.